HOW THE
ECONOMY
WORKS

HOW THE
ECONOMY
WORKS
An Investor's Guide to Tracking the Economy

Edmund A. Mennis

New York Institute of Finance
New York   London   Toronto   Sydney   Tokyo   Singapore

Library of Congress Cataloging-in-Publication Data

Mennis, Edmund A., 1919–
    How the economy works / by Edmund A. Mennis.
        p.   cm.
    Includes index.
    ISBN 0-13-401035-3
    1. Economics.   2. United States—Economic conditions—1981–
3. Investments.   I. Title.
HB171.M523   1991
332.6'78—dc20   91-23182
                                                                      CIP

This publication is designed to provide accurate and
authoritative information in regard to the subject matter
covered. It is sold with the understanding that the publisher
is not engaged in rendering legal, accounting, or other
professional service. If legal advice or other expert
assistance is required, the services of a competent
professional person should be sought.

From a Declaration of Principles
Jointly Adopted by
a Committee of the American Bar Association
and a Committee of Publishers and Associations

Printed in the United States of America

10 9 8 7 6 5 4 3

Contents

CHAPTER 12
Suggestions for the Individual Investor, 243

Preface

How the Economy Works: An Investor's Guide to Tracking the Economy originated from a series of brief reports prepared for my clients designed to explain and interpret the current batch of statistics available in the financial press. I soon discovered that the biggest problem was a lack of understanding of the vast statistical data system the United States has developed and the technical terminology used to report it. Consequently, I started another series of reports explaining the various statistical series and how they told us what was going on in the economy. When three years of these reports had accumulated,

I was urged to put them together in a book; *How the Economy Works* is the result. *Note: An explanation of the abbreviations used in the source notes to the figures can be found in the reference section at the end of the book.*

I want to express my appreciation to Sheshunoff Information Services, who permitted me to use some of the material in the chapter "Managing Trust Investments" that I wrote for their *Trust Department Management Manual.* I am grateful to Dr. Carol Carson, Deputy Director, Bureau of Economic Analysis, U.S. Department of Commerce, for permission to use Figure 9.5, taken from the *Survey of Current Business.* She also kindly provided a copy of the chart for reproduction. I also appreciate the willingness of staff members of the Bureau of Economic Analysis, the Bureau of the Census, the Bureau of Labor Statistics, the Social Security Administration, the Congressional Budget Office, the Research Department of the Board of Governors of the Federal Reserve System, and the National Association of Purchasing Management to provide me with historical data not readily available in standard reference sources.

My greatest obligation is to my wife, Tres, and my son, Liam. They not only encouraged me to undertake the writing of this book, but, in addition, critically read every chapter. Their unrelenting insistence that I delete economic jargon and write in plain English has, I hope, made the book more readable. If I have failed in that, the fault certainly is not theirs. My debt to them is substantial.

Edmund A. Mennis

Palos Verdes Estates, CA
April 1991

CHAPTER 1

Why Bother About the Economy?

Each day, we are subjected to a lot of economic information, whether from newspapers, radio, or television. This information is just a small piece of a very complicated mosaic that makes up the economy, and it may be expressed in technical jargon that is difficult for the uninitiated to understand. Economic information often appears obscure and confusing, and it is little wonder that the average individual questions whether it's worth trying to understand how the economy works.

Understanding the health of the U.S. economy is very important if we are to be better informed citizens and voters. Moreover, knowledge of the economy may influence a choice of careers or a change in jobs. Fluctuations in the economy affect the stability of a job. Understanding how the economy works also helps to make sound investment decisions.

Most people are constantly making decisions about what to consume and how to invest. "Investment" is a word often used to mean just buying and selling stocks, an exercise that many individuals have little or nothing to do with. Many more investment decisions other than buying or selling stocks are made every day. For example, investment decisions are made when buying or refinancing a home and deciding whether to use a fixed- or variable-rate mortgage. Buying high-ticket items and paying either with cash or credit is an investment decision. Taking out a personal loan is an investment decision; so is deciding whether to put money aside in a savings account, a money-market fund, a bank certificate of deposit, or a U.S. Treasury bond. All of these decisions are influenced by movements in interest rates, which in turn are affected by movements in the economy.

Future income may be affected by changes in the economy. The value of a pension plan is affected by changes in interest rates and stock prices. While this may not be too important if pension benefits are set by salary levels and years of service, it is critical if retirement benefits are related to the market value of a pension, profit sharing, or thrift plan. Some employee benefit plans offer a selection, allowing a combination of investments—and that combination may be changed from time to time. What are the best choices at any given time? It may not be last year's best investment performer.

The list could go on, but the point is clear. Everyone makes decisions that affects his or her future economic well-being. These decisions will improve with a better understanding of where the economy is, where it is going, and how to track its changes. The goal of this book is to make that task easier.

ECONOMICS AND THE ECONOMY

Economics is the social science that deals with the allocation of scarce resources. It is concerned chiefly with the description and analysis of the production, distribution, and consumption of goods and services. However, this book is not designed to be an economics text; it has other objectives.

This book is intended to enable the reader to understand and interpret the flood of economic information provided by the news media, government, and private sources. A good deal more economic information is available; just coping with economic information covered in the financial press is a sufficiently ambitious task.

A major challenge in understanding current data is to put it in some sort of perspective. The latest information may be expressed as a percentage change from last month or a year ago. Looking back over a period longer than a month, is the trend of the data up, down, or indeterminate? How does this information relate to other information at hand? How does this information provide a perspective of what is going on in the whole economy? Is business getting better or worse?

One method of providing needed perspective is to plot the data on a chart to show the movements for a period of several years or longer. Consequently, this book has many figures. Remember, the figures are as important as the text; it is worthwhile to spend a few minutes looking at each, trying to understand the story it has to tell.

If it is important to know how the economy affects us, where does one start? A basic assumption is the logical relationship that flows from the economy to corporate profits, and from those profits to stock prices. The path of the economy also influences interest rates. This chapter will develop these relationships.

The following terms are introduced in this chapter:

Gross national product (GNP). The measure of the output of goods and services in the economy;

Corporate profits. The estimate of the current income received by corporations as a part of the income generated by GNP;

Standard & Poor's 500 (S&P 500) Stock Price Index and *S&P earnings per share*. The combined prices and earnings of a group of 500 large, successful corporations;

Price-earnings (P/E) ratio. The price of a stock divided by its past or expected earnings, indicating how many years of earnings a particular price represents. A similar relationship can be calculated for groups of stocks, like the S&P 500;

Interest rates. The dollars of interest income received per $100 of investment.

ARE THE ECONOMY AND INVESTMENTS RELATED?

At this point, would a better understanding of the economy help make better investment decision possible? Are the economy and investment decisions related? If so, how?

Movements in the economy, in corporate profits, and in stock prices are related. The economy and interest rates are also connected. The following figures provide examples of relationships between economic information and the movement of stock prices and interest rates.

The figures cover a long period of time—from 1950, just after World War II, to 1990. This 41-year period was different from the years prior to World War II in terms of economic growth rates and cyclical fluctuations. It also encompassed the Korean and Vietnam wars, two oil shocks that led to bursts of very high inflation, and population shifts that changed the allocation of scarce economic resources. This longer-term viewpoint should provide the needed perspective to evaluate the transitory developments and the external shocks that often heavily influence investment decisions.

The Economy and Corporate Profits

Figure 1.1 compares *gross national product* (GNP), the broadest measure of the output of goods and services in the United States, with the *corporate profits* generated from that output. These two measures will be examined in more detail in Chapters 2 and 10, but for now we just want to demonstrate that the movements of the economy and of profits are related. GNP is expressed in current dollars—reflecting both move-

Figure 1.1.   GNP and Profits

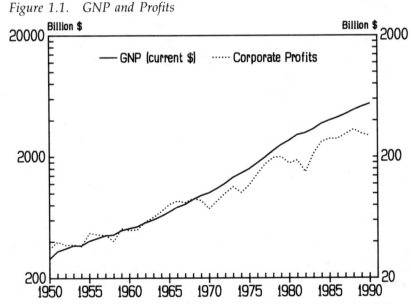

Source: Current data for GNP: SCB, February 1991, Table 1.1, p. 7. Profits: SCB, February 1991, Table 1.14, p. 9. Earlier data ERP 1991, Table B-1, page 286 and Table B-24, p. 313.

ments in physical output and changes in prices. The measure of corporate profits used here is called *operating profits* or *economic profits*. These profit numbers are an estimate of all corporate profits in the economy before state and federal taxes. They are adjusted to eliminate the effects on profits of fluctuations in the value of the inventories corporations carry on their books. These profit numbers also are adjusted to show the depreciation of corporate plant and equipment to reflect current rather than historical costs. Thus, this profit measure is the one most directly related to current output.

A word about the method of presentation in Figure 1.1. GNP is measured by the scale on the left side of the figure. This scale is ten times the right scale, which is used to measure operating profits. These dual scales are used to bring the lines on the figure closer together so that they can be compared more easily. The vertical axes of the figure are set so that vertical distances on the chart show equal *percentage* changes rather than equal dollar changes. Note, for example, on the left scale, the distance from 200 to 2,000 (an increase of 1,800) is equal to the distance from 2,000 to 20,000 (an increase of 18,000). However, both distances represent a 900 percent increase. Such a figure, called a *semilog chart*, permits better comparisons of variables that differ widely in amount.

Several observations can be made about the data on these figures. First, the economy and profits appear to be related; they both have had a broad upward sweep. However, the trend of profits has not been so steep as that of the economy, suggesting that the profit share of output has not kept pace with overall economic growth. Part of the reason for this difference is the rising share of employee compensation, especially fringe benefits, that has grown as a percent of total output. The second reason is the increase in indebtedness of U.S. corporations, resulting in interest costs that have claimed an increasing share of corporate output.

Another difference is clearly evident. Profits fluctuate a good deal more than the economy as a whole (remember that equal vertical distances on the figure represent equal percentage changes). These fluctuations are due to periodic fluctuations in the economy called *business cycles*. Business cycles are an economic phenomenon that affect different sectors of the economy in varying ways (more about business cycles in Chapter 9). The point made here is that business cycles affect profits, and anyone interested in profits needs a better understanding of cyclical fluctuations in the economy.

STOCK EARNINGS AND PRICES

Figure 1.2 examines the relationship between corporate profits or earnings and the prices of the stocks of the companies

Figure 1.2.   S&P Earnings and Prices

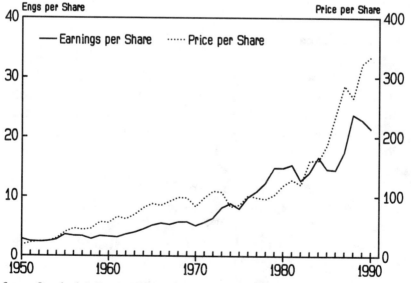

Source: Standard & Poor's Trade and Statistics Manual, Standard & Poor's Corporation, New York, NY, pps. 1, 115–118.

that generated those earnings. (The economic profits for all corporations shown in Figure 1.1 and the earnings per share for the stocks in the Standard & Poor's 500 stock index shown in Figure 1.2 have had generally similar fluctuations over time. The Standard & Poor's index is comprised of 500 large, successful corporations; this index is used in order to compare earnings and stock prices of the same companies.) The scales of the figure have been constructed so that the price scale on the right side is ten times the earnings scale on the left side.

Several factors are evident in this figure. Although prices have been more volatile than earnings, both have trended upward in a similar manner to growth in the economy. The position of the price line above and below the earnings line not only indicates that prices are more volatile, but that they also move in broad patterns around the earnings line, sometimes higher and sometimes lower. Stock prices are fundamentally related to earnings but the prices that investors are willing to pay for these earnings change from time to time.

The Price/Earnings Ratio

The relationship between prices and earnings is shown more clearly by the solid line on Figure 1.3. Data for the solid line were computed by dividing the annual earnings of the S&P 500 stock index by the average price each year, resulting in what investors call the *price/earnings ratio*, shown on the scale at the left of the chart.

Several distinct patterns are found in this ratio. Prices moved from a low of about 7 times earnings in 1950 to a peak of more than 22 times in 1962. Except for that one year, the ratio fluctuated between about 14.5 times to just under 19 times between 1959 and 1972. The decline thereafter was sharp, and the ratio moved between 7 to 11 times until 1984. Since then the ratio has generally fluctuated within 12 to 16 times. The aver-

Figure 1.3.   Stock P/E Ratios and Inflation

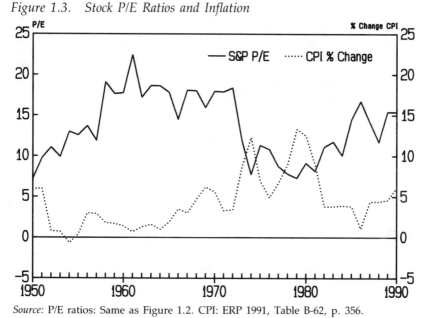

Source: P/E ratios: Same as Figure 1.2. CPI: ERP 1991, Table B-62, p. 356.

age P/E ratio for the entire 1950 to 1990 period was about 13.7 times.

Why has this ratio, which represents the value thousands of investors have placed on corporate earnings, fluctuated this way? Although a number of explanations can be advanced, one simple relationship is significant. The dotted line on the figure shows the annual change in the *consumer price index (CPI)*—one method often used to measure inflation. The inflation rate averaged less than 2 percent from 1950 to 1963, which was a period of rising P/E ratios and thus rising valuation of earnings by investors. The costs of the Vietnam War and the two oil price shocks in the 1970s led to a surge in inflation, slower growth in corporate earnings, and a sharp downward revision in P/E ratios. The recession and deflation that began in 1982 drove inflation rates under 4 percent, which had a salutary effect on stock price multiples, sending them up again.

In summary, growth and cyclical fluctuations in the economy affect corporate profits, and the inflation rate has a strong influence on the valuation investors place on those earnings. Knowledge of what makes the economy move and the causes of and changes in inflation rates can help to explain broad movements in stock prices as well as assist in making better investment decisions.

INTEREST RATES

The importance of interest rate movements in making investment decisions was mentioned earlier in this chapter. Figure 1.4 provides a long-term view of the movement of both short- and long-term *interest rates* for the 1950 to 1990 period.

Figure 1.4.   Short- and Long-Term Interest Rates

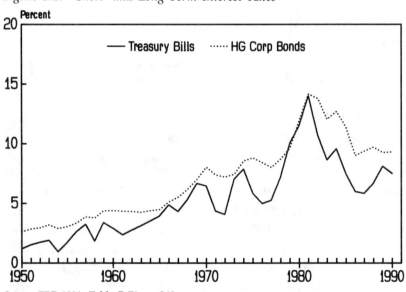

Source: ERP 1991, Table B-71, p. 368.

(Interest rates are expressed as a percent, computed by the dollars of interest received per $100 of investment. The value of the investment is ordinarily expressed in terms of its market price.) Short rates are measured by the yield on 30-day U.S. Treasury bills. Many short-term rates, like those on bank certificates of deposit (CDs) and savings accounts, are directly related to the Treasury bill rate; they are a part of the holdings of many money-market mutual funds. Long-term rates are represented by yields of high-grade corporate bonds. This information is prepared regularly by the investment firm of Salomon Brothers.

Two interesting characteristics of interest rates may be observed from this figure. The first is that short rates have been more volatile than long rates. In fact, an analysis of the monthly movements in short-term interest rates would reveal that short-term rates have relatively large movements that conform to cyclical fluctuations in the economy. Turning points in long rates lag behind short-rate turns and have smaller amplitudes. Moreover, near cyclical business-cycle peaks, short rates tend to exceed long rates, resulting in a so-called inverted yield curve, which will be discussed in Chapter 8. Presumably these movements reflect different supply and demand forces affecting these securities, and these forces are related to the economic conditions prevailing in these particular years.

The second characteristic is the trends of both short and long rates during this period. Both rates trended upward from 1950 to 1981 but fell thereafter. A possible explanation of these trends is the same force that affected stock P/E ratios. Figure 1.5 plots the fluctuations in the Treasury bill rate (the solid line) against the annual changes in the consumer price index (the bars). As a generalization, the bill rate has fluctuated almost consistently with the annual inflation rate, running slightly above it in the earlier years, and below it in periods of high inflation. Since 1981, however, the bill rate has run considera-

Figure 1.5.   Interest Rates and Inflation

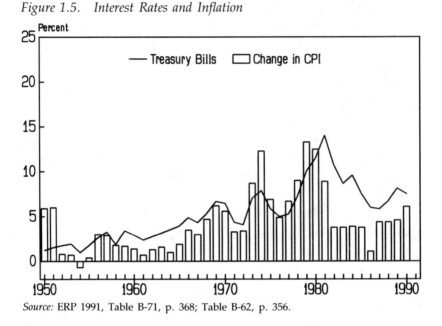

Source: ERP 1991, Table B-71, p. 368; Table B-62, p. 356.

bly above the inflation rate. This latter phenomenon suggests either investors in recent years have demanded a higher return above inflation than in earlier periods or they anticipate even higher inflation rates in the future. In any event, knowledge of the stage of the business cycle and the prospects for inflation can be important in evaluating interest rate prospects.

SUMMARY

Knowing how to interpret fluctuations in the economy is important. All investment decisions are impacted by changes in the economy—including those that don't involve buying and selling stocks.

Movements in corporate profits are related to movements in the economy. Stock prices are consequently affected by profit movements and the price that investors are willing to pay for these profits. This relationship is reflected in the P/E ratio; the P/E ratio is influenced as a result of changes in inflation rates. Interest rates are also related to fluctuations in the economy, and trends in interest rates are related to trends in inflation rates.

Thus, economics and investments are intertwined. A better understanding of the economy will lead to a better understanding of the major influences on investment returns. It will also reduce the influence on your business and investment decisions of the minor or extraneous factors that loom large in newspaper headlines.

CHAPTER 2

What Is GNP Anyway?

Understanding the economy involves unraveling a confusing flood of statistics and conflicting opinions of economists interpreting these statistics. This chapter attempts to sort out the statistical confusion first; the confusing economists are dealt with later.

The easiest way to explain the economy is to start with the "Big Picture" and examine the broadest measure of economic activity available, or gross national product (GNP). After discussing the dual concept of GNP, the economy can then be analyzed later in terms of each of the major components of GNP: the consumer, business, government, and the international sector. Under each of these four divisions, other statistical data will be discussed that, in addition to GNP and its parts, provide useful insights into each sector. Hopefully, a more comprehensible picture of the operation of the economy will emerge.

Among the terms introduced in this chapter are:

Gross national product. A measure that estimates the *output* of goods and services in the economy and also the *income* generated by that output of goods and services;

Final sales. That portion of GNP that is taken by the ultimate user. Final sales are made to consumers, government, and foreigners; they are reflected in business spending for plant and equipment as well as new residential housing sales;

Changes in business inventories. The additions to or reductions in business holdings of inventories. When these changes in inventories are combined with final sales, the result is total GNP;

Income side of GNP. Includes employee compensation and the interest paid by business (less the interest it receives), plus corporate profits, incomes of proprietorships and partnerships, and rental income of persons.

WHAT IS GNP?

GNP is a part of the national income and product accounts (NIPA) prepared and distributed by the federal government. The process is similiar to a corporation keeping books with income and balance sheet accounts reflecting the health of the corporation. However, GNP accounts are much broader in scope; they are designed to show the production, distribution, and use of the nation's output of goods and services. A full set of the national accounts includes some 130 tables of statistical information with some 4,200 items, and much of the information is of interest primarily to those who specialize in a particular area.

This chapter will cover only the major parts of the GNP accounts and will explain how the limited GNP data reported in the press or on TV can be interpreted to understand the status of the economy.

Definitions

GNP can be measured in two ways:

How the output of goods and services in any particular time period is apportioned among various users of the output; or

How the income generated by that output of goods and services is distributed.

The measurement of the output of goods and services reflects *final sales* to the ultimate user only; sales at intermediate stages of production are excluded.[1] If the *changes in business inventories* (either additions or reductions) are added to final sales, we get total GNP or output.

---

[1]The purpose of this exclusion is to avoid multiple counting. For example, iron ore is used to make steel, which is used to make bicycles. If the iron ore is counted when it is first mined, again as a part of the content of the steel and then again as a part of the steel in the bicycle, it would be counted several times. The price of the bicycle when it is finally sold includes the value of the iron ore and the other materials used in manufacture as well as the value added at each stage of production.

18

THE OUTPUT SIDE OF GNP

Final sales are made to four sectors:

1. Sales to consumers;

2. Sales representing gross fixed investment, that is, plant and equipment spending by business plus new residential housing sales;

3. Sales to government, defined as compensation of government employees and government purchases from business and abroad;

4. Sales to foreigners, that is, exports less imports of goods and services. By definition imports are of foreign rather than domestic production; therefore they are subtracted to get a measure of the production attributable to the United States.

Table 2.1 shows GNP in 1990 and how it was taken off the market by the four sectors.

As the table indicates, the consumer takes the largest portion of the nation's output, about two-thirds. Government

Table 2.1.
How GNP Was Taken Off the Market—1990

	Billions of $	Percent
Total GNP	$5,463.6	100.0
Personal Consumption Expenditures	3,658.6	67.0
Nonresidential Fixed Investment	523.7	9.6
Residential Fixed Investment	222.4	4.1
Change in Business Inventories	− 4.2	−0.1
Government Purchases of Goods and Services	1,097.8	20.1
Net Exports	− 34.6	−0.6

takes the next largest slice, about 20 percent. Business fixed investment (structures as well as machinery and equipment) and business accumulation (or reduction) of inventories follow with about 10 percent. The residential investment—the value of on-site construction of single-family homes, multiple dwellings and of mobile homes (4 percent) follows. (The figure does not represent sales to homebuyers but rather outlays for construction during the period being measured.) Finally, net exports are a negative sum because in the United States in 1990, domestic consumption of goods and services imported was greater than goods and services exported.

One other note about the way GNP is reported. Each month the reports show GNP and its components at *seasonally adjusted annual rates*. Seasonal adjustment is a statistical technique that makes allowances for seasonal patterns in activity caused by weather patterns or predictable surges due to events such as Christmas or Easter shopping. Showing the figures at annual rates indicates the degree of change for a whole year if the change in a particular quarter continued for a year at that rate. This way of presenting the information makes it possible to compare the data for a calendar quarter with that for an entire year.

Data for GNP are reported reflecting prices that prevailed in the reporting period. This information is referred to as *current dollar* or *nominal* GNP. In order to get a measure of change in physical output, the Commerce Department also computes GNP expressed in prices that prevailed in 1982, called *real* GNP, *constant dollar* GNP, or *inflation-adjusted* GNP. Dividing nominal GNP by a price index measures the physical volume of output, because prices are held constant. At present, prices of GNP and its components in 1982 are used as the divisor, so that real GNP is expressed in terms of constant 1982 prices. Computation of the GNP price indexes is discussed in Chapter 3.

Table 2.2 compares GNP in 1990 expressed in constant 1982 dollars as well as in current dollars, as was shown in Table 2.1.

The differences in the percentages for the various components shown in the current and constant dollar columns reflect prices rising faster in some components than in others. For example, personal consumption expenditures in 1990 accounted for 64.5 percent of GNP measured in 1982 prices but 67 percent measured in current prices. This difference reflects personal consumption prices increasing faster than prices of GNP as a whole from 1982 to 1990.

THE INCOME SIDE OF GNP

Another way of looking at GNP is to consider it as the sum of incomes generated in producing the nation's output. These incomes comprise:

The cost of production; and

Profits.

The costs of producing the nation's output goods and services are:

Employee compensation; and

The interest paid by business less the interest it receives.

The profits part of incomes consists of:

Corporate profits;

Incomes of proprietorships and partnerships; and

Rental income received by persons.

Table 2.2.
GNP for 1990 in Current and Constant 1982 Dollars

	Current Dollars	Percent	1982 Dollars	Percent
Total GNP	$5,463.6	100.0	4,156.3	100.0
Personal Consumption Expenditures	3,658.6	67.0	2,682.4	64.5
Nonresidential Fixed Investment	523.7	9.6	515.0	12.4
Residential Fixed Investment	222.4	4.1	177.1	4.3
Change in Business Inventories	− 4.2	−0.1	− 2.5	—
Government Purchases of Goods and Services	1,097.8	20.1	820.5	19.7
Net Exports	− 34.6	−0.6	− 36.2	−0.9

However, before national income can be distributed, some adjustments are necessary. First, an allowance must be made for the current cost of the capital used up in production (a measure of the depreciation of plant and equipment). When these charges are subtracted from GNP, the result is called *net national product*. Then indirect business taxes charged as a business expense (sales, excise, and business property taxes) are subtracted. A few other minor adjustments—accounting in total less that 1 percent of GNP—are made. They include business transfer payments (mostly business charitable deductions and consumer bad debts) and a statistical discrepancy to absorb the unexplained differences between the income and product side of the accounts. The resulting figure is called *national income*, which is then distributed between the costs of production and profits.

Table 2.3 shows the income distribution of GNP in 1990.

As Table 2.3 indicates, the distribution of national income is more than 80 percent of total GNP. Almost 60 percent is employee compensation, which is composed of:

Wages and salaries, both in the private sector and also salaries of employees of government and government enterprises;

Supplements to wages and salaries, including employee contributions to social insurance. (In 1990, these supplementary payments represented more than 16 percent of total employee compensation.)

The second production cost, net interest, reflects the interest paid by business as a part of its operations, less interest received.

The profits figure has two components: corporate profits and proprietors' income from farm and nonfarm business. Both of these components receive a relatively small proportion of

Table 2.3.
Income Distribution of GNP—1990

	Billions of Dollars	Percent
Total GNP	$5,463.6	100.0
Less: Capital Consumption Allowances	575.6	10.5
Net National Product	4,888.0	89.5
Less: Indirect Business Taxes	440.3	8.1
Statistical Discrepancy	− 3.1	—
Other Adjustments	32.5	0.6
National Income	4,418.2	80.8
Distributed as Follows:		
Production Costs:		
Employee Compensation	$3,244.2	59.4
Net Interest Received by Business	466.6	8.5
Profits:		
Corporate Profits	298.7	5.5
Proprietorships and Partnerships	402.2	7.3
Rental Income of Persons	6.5	0.1

national income, and proprietorship income is larger than corporate profits. These profits are before income taxes.

The final payment, rental income to persons, represents rent from farm and nonfarm residential as well as nonresidential properties; it also includes royalties reported on individual income tax returns. This payment accounts for a relatively small part of national income.

REVISIONS

A complete record of every economic transaction that takes place in the United States does not exist. In addition, information becomes available at different times, often with a considerable time lag. Therefore, the numbers for GNP and its components (and for most economic statistics, for that matter) are estimates, the reliability of which generally improves over time. The GNP data provided by the government are a compromise between the need for prompt information and the desire for accuracy. Some data are more reliable than others; for example, the dollar value of new car sales is more accurate than the dollars spent on motor vehicle repair, washing, parking, and rental. Some data are little more than educated guesses (e.g., the estimated rent of owner-occupied dwellings). Consequently, the accuracy of the numbers should not be taken too literally and certainly not believed to the last decimal place!

Quarterly GNP estimates are published each month, generally between the 23rd and the 29th day of the month. The first estimate for a particular quarter—the *advance estimate*—is published in the first month of the following quarter; for example, the first estimate of the first quarter is published at the end of April. The second estimate, the *revised estimate*, is published a month later, and the third or *final estimate* is published in the third month of the succeeding quarter.

Each July, the data for the previous three years are revised based on more complete information and on data available only on an annual basis. Finally, every five years or so a complete overhaul is done to include information from the periodic surveys the government makes of the economy. Even with a statistical reporting system considered one of the best in the world, it should not be surprising that revisions in where the economy *was* are partly responsible for the difficulties economists encounter in estimating where the economy *is going*.

BUSINESS ANALYSIS

Unfortunately, the quarterly reports of GNP published in the press and on television hardly provide the depth and wealth of information the full releases contain. Usually, only a brief comment on the quarter-to-quarter change in real GNP is reported, perhaps accompanied by a comment on the change in prices during that period.

However, even this brief information has some analytical value, especially if successive estimates are tracked for a particular quarter to determine whether the economy seems to be getting stronger or weaker. For example, the initial report of the quarterly change in GNP for the fourth quarter of 1987 (the big stock market crash occurred in October) was an increase of 4.2 percent at an annual rate, quite a bit better than had been expected. And in the next two months, the estimate was revised to show gains of 4.5 and 4.8 percent, respectively, indicating that the market crash did not paralyze the economy as many had feared. (As a matter of fact, the July 1990 revisions of GNP for the past three years now show estimated growth at an estimated rate of 6.6 percent for the fourth quarter of 1987!)

Another very important factor to remember in interpreting economic reports is not attaching too much significance to quarter-to-quarter or month-to-month changes. Movements over several years should be reviewed in order to get an impression of the general direction of the series being examined.

As an example, Figure 2.1 shows the quarterly percent change in inflation-adjusted GNP from the first quarter of 1986 to fourth quarter of 1990. This figure provides a vivid comparison of the 1989 to 1990 quarters with those in 1986. The small drop in the second quarter of 1986 was followed by a number of quarters of strong growth. By contrast, beginning in the second quarter of 1989 growth continued at a low annual rate of less than 2 percent. This prolonged weakness of the economy is a prelude to a business contraction that is evident in the fourth quarter of 1990.

The demand components of the quarterly GNP estimates are usually provided in the business section of the daily news-

Figure 2.1.   Real Gross National Product % Change

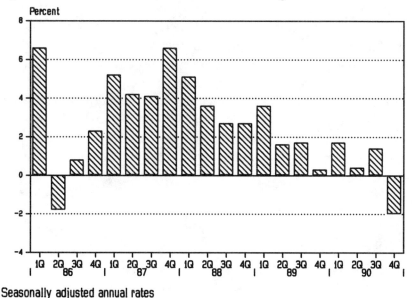

Seasonally adjusted annual rates

Source: SCB, February 1991, Table 1.2, p. 7; earlier data ERP 1991, Table B-5, p. 293.

papers, and an examination of the changes can provide clues to the cyclical position of the economy. The details of these components will be considered in Chapters 4, 5, 6, and 7.

SUMMARY

This chapter described GNP, the broadest measure of economic activity in the economy. This measure is comprised of two parts: the product side and the income side. GNP is also reported in current prices and adjusted for price changes to provide a measure of the physical volume of output (as discussed in Chapter 3).

Quarterly details of GNP at an annual rate are made available each month. The advance estimate is available toward the end of the month following the close of the quarter. A revised estimate is published a month later, followed by the final estimate in the third month. A complete revision covering the previous three years is published each July. These revisions, as well as those of many other economic data, make it difficult to know where the economy is and thus more difficult to predict.

For business analysis, the primary focus should be on the output or product side. Tracking the quarterly percentage changes as well as the revisions should be reviewed in the perspective of several years of changes. Analysis of the components of demand can provide clues to the future cyclical path of the economy.

CHAPTER 3

Measuring Price Changes

In Chapter 2 it was stated that GNP expressed in current prices could be converted to a physical volume measure if it were divided by an index representing prices in a particular year. That index is discussed in this chapter.

Price indexes serve a more important function than just adjusting current dollar GNP. One of the key issues facing the United States in the years ahead is the outlook for inflation. *Inflation* is a slippery word, meaning different things to different people. However, the most commonly accepted definition is a period of accelerating price increases. Why are price changes important, and how are they measured?

This chapter will cover all three price indexes that have been developed for measuring price changes in the GNP accounts. In addition, two other measures of prices that are more widely known and used than those in the GNP accounts are discussed.

The specific indexes discussed are:

GNP *implicit price deflator.* An index that is the broadest measure of prices in the economy, reflecting the prices prevailing in a particular period (calendar quarter or year), weighted by the composition of GNP in that period;

Fixed-weight price index for GNP. Reflects the level of prices for a particular period, assuming that the composition of GNP did not change from that in a base period, currently the year 1982;

Chain-price index for GNP. This index shows how prices reflect the assumption that the composition of GNP was unchanged from the first of two consecutive periods;

Consumer price index. Reflects the prices a typical consumer pays for a fixed-market basket of consumer goods and services;

Producer price indexes. Prices received by domestic producers of commodities at three stages of processing—crude materials, intermediate materials, and finished goods.

WHY ARE PRICE CHANGES IMPORTANT?

Price changes, especially price increases, are important for several reasons. Rising (or falling) prices introduce inequities into the economy. The ability to offset rising prices varies; for example, those receiving periodic payments in a specific number of dollars are hurt if their payments are not indexed to inflation. These include private pension fund recipients or persons who own securities where the income payments are fixed, such as bonds or savings accounts or certificates of deposit. In a period of rising prices, the purchasing power of the fixed amounts they receive is eroded. The inequities within the economy are magnified if other fixed payments are adjusted for inflation through law (as in the case of social security payments) or contract (as in the case of cost-of-living adjustments in labor contracts).

In addition to the inequities that arise when prices change, a relationship exists over time between prices and wages. The dotted line on Figure 3.1 shows the annual changes of the consumer price index less food and fuel prices from 1958

Figure 3.1.   Prices and Wages

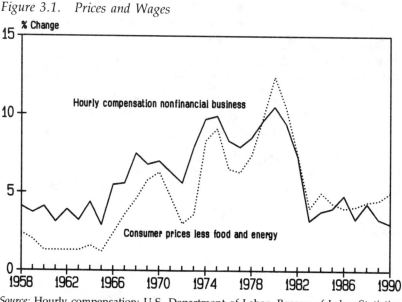

Source: Hourly compensation: U.S. Department of Labor, Bureau of Labor Statistics release *Productivity and Costs,* various dates. CPI: ERP 1991, Table B-61, p. 355.

through 1990. (Food and fuel prices are subtracted because they are so volatile, depending on the weather in the case of food and on the whims of foreign oil producers, in the case of fuel. The index less food and fuel prices is often referred to as the *core inflation rate*.) The solid line indicates the annual changes in hourly compensation of employees in nonfinancial corporations. Although the correspondence is not precise, clearly in the period of generally rising prices from 1965 to 1980 compensation tracked the price rises, and increases in compensation slowed when prices declined after 1980. Moreover, the cyclical patterns of both series were similar.

Although wages may lag behind price changes, wages inevitably go up as prices go up, because labor attempts to maintain its share of national income. The lags in adjustment add to the distortions in the economy in the short run. In addition, higher labor costs add to pressures for higher prices, setting a vicious cycle in motion.

Even the fear of inflation is so worrisome that it has become a major concern of the U.S. monetary authority, the Federal Reserve (Fed). Consequently, signs of inflation usually result in tighter monetary policy, causing higher interest rates. Because of this emphasis on price changes, it may be helpful to understand the measures available to monitor prices, so that they can both be followed, understood, and interpreted.

As expected, the broadest measures of price changes are associated with the broadest measure of economic activity, the GNP. In addition, several other price measures are available, some of which are probably better known than the GNP price measures. We shall examine all of them in the remainder of this chapter.

GNP PRICE MEASURES

A good portion of the numbers in the GNP accounts are expressed in *current* prices. An estimate is also made of GNP and its components in *constant* or *real* dollars, that is, estimates from which price changes have been removed. For these real estimates, each GNP component is valued at its price in a base valuation period (this base year is updated from time-to-time; currently it is 1982). When a quantity of GNP or one of its components expressed in current prices is divided by a quantity expressed in 1982 prices, the quantities cancel and you have current prices divided by 1982 prices, or a price index in which 1982 is equal to 100. Because this price index is derived in this fashion rather than directly by adding up the prices of all of the items in the index, it is called an *implicit price deflator*. This price index reflects both price changes and changes in the distribution of the components of GNP; it does not reflect changes in prices alone.

A second GNP price index, *fixed-weight price index*, is also prepared. In this index, the price components are weighted by the composition or percentage distribution of GNP in 1982, assuming no subsequent changes in the proportionate distribution. Therefore, changes in this index reflect the effects of price changes alone. However, moving further away from the base year, these price changes become inadequate representations of prices in the current economy, because the composition of GNP has shifted. At times the press reports on changes in the implicit price deflator; at other times the fixed-weight index is reported. It is important to distinguish between the two in order to know what is being measured.

A third GNP index prepared is called the *chain price index*. It is a weighted average of the same detailed price indexes, but they are combined by using the weights that reflect the composition of GNP in the first of two consecutive periods. For example, the chain price index for the fourth quarter of 1988 reflects the changes in prices in the fourth quarter if the composition of GNP had not changed from the third quarter. This index is the least used of the three because it permits comparison between only two years or two calendar quarters.

THE CONSUMER PRICE INDEX

The price index most familiar to the average consumer and investor is the *consumer price index (CPI)*. This index is the one used to adjust social security payments as well as labor and other contracts with a cost-of-living adjustment. The index is supposed to reflect the changes in the prices the typical consumer pays over time for a fixed-market basket of consumer goods and services. The CPI for all urban consumers represents spending patterns for about 80 percent of the noninstitutional population. The index is based on prices for food, clothing, shelter and fuels, transportation fares, charges for doctors' and dentists' services, drugs, and other goods and services that people buy for day-to-day living.[1]

Prices are collected in 91 urban areas across the country from about 60,000 housing units and 21,000 retail establishments. Prices of food, fuels, and a few other items are collected every month in all 91 locations. Prices of all other commodities and services are collected every month in the five largest geographic areas and every other month in other areas.

Figure 3.2 provides a breakdown of the composition of the CPI in December 1989. Housing costs are the largest component of the index. The 28 percent shown in the pie chart for shelter includes rents or homeowners' equivalent of rent, household insurance, and maintenance and repairs. Other household costs are for fuels and other utilities (7 percent) and house furnishings, housekeeping supplies and services (7 percent). All told, household costs account for 42 percent of total

[1]This index is technically called CPI-U. Another index, CPI-W, is also issued. It represents urban wage and clerical workers employed in blue-collar occupations. It accounts for a smaller (only 32 percent) of the noninstitutional population, and it is not used as much as the CPI-U index.

Figure 3.2.   Components of Consumer Price Index

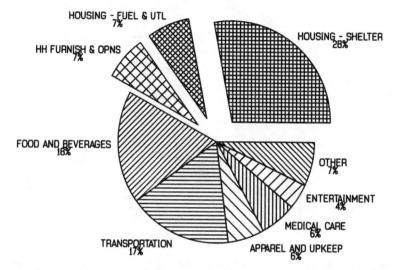

HOUSING – FUEL & UTL
7%

HH FURNISH & OPNS
7%

HOUSING – SHELTER
28%

FOOD AND BEVERAGES
18%

OTHER
7%

ENTERTAINMENT
4%

MEDICAL CARE
6%

TRANSPORTATION
17%

APPAREL AND UPKEEP
6%

Source: CPI Detailed Report, U.S. Department of Labor, Bureau of Labor Statistics, December 1990, p. 62.

consumer expenditures. In addition, food and beverages account for 18 percent of consumer expenditures, apparel and upkeep account for 6 percent, transportation for 17 percent, medical care for 6 percent, entertainment for 4 percent, and other goods and services the remaining 7 percent. In 1988, the components were shifted to reflect consumer purchasing patterns in 1982 through 1984 instead of 1967.

Figure 3.3 provides a perspective of the annual changes in consumer prices for most of the time since World War II, the 41-year period from 1950 through 1990. For this entire period, the average annual price increase was 4.4 percent. However, in this case, the average conceals some very interesting differences. The average annual increase from 1950 to 1965 was a low 2.0 percent. The Vietnam War effects on the economy caused prices to more than double for the 1966 to 1972 period. Two oil

Figure 3.3.   Consumer Price Index 1950–90

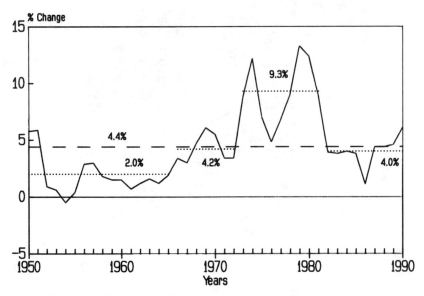

Source: ERP 1991, Table B-60, p. 354. Computations by author.

price shocks sent prices soaring in the 1973 to 1981 period, when the average annual price increase was more than 9 percent, with several years well above that level. The business contractions of 1980 and 1981 to 1982 as well as the restrictive monetary policies of that period caused prices to fall considerably, so that in 1982 to 1990 price increases averaged 4.0 percent, but in 1990 were above that level. As for the future, the long-term outlook for inflation as well as the economy will be considered in Chapter 9.

Figure 3.3 provides a background against which monthly price reports can be evaluated. However, regular press reports on consumer prices usually focus on the month-to-month price changes—and these numbers may seem deceptively small. After all, a monthly gain of 0.3 or 0.4 percent may not seem like much. A more useful piece of information usually included in most press reports is the percentage rise in prices over the past 12 months, which then can be compared with the annual changes in Figure 3.3.

But even this additional information may not provide an appropriate perspective. Year-to-year changes as shown in Figure 3.3 do not reflect the cumulative effects of price increases over a longer period of time. Figure 3.4 illustrates this point. An average annual inflation rate of 4.3 percent may not seem like a lot, but the devastating effect on the value of the currency is shown by the fact that a $1 in 1950 had lost more than 80 percent of its purchasing power by 1990 and was worth about nineteen cents!

Figure 3.4. Purchasing Power of a 1950 Dollar

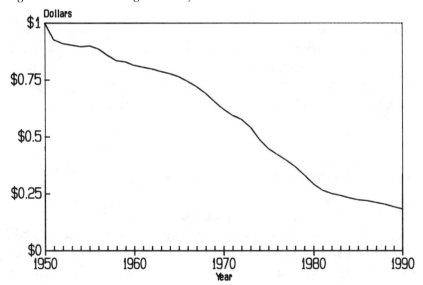

Source: ERP 1991, Table B-60, p. 354. Computations by the author.

PRODUCER PRICE INDEXES

A third group of price indexes reflects prices of products only, not services. These indexes reflect prices received by domestic producers of commodities at all stages of processing. The base reference period in the index is 1982 prices set to equal 100. About 31,000 commodities and 75,000 price quotations are obtained each month.

Actually, price indexes are prepared for three separate stages of production: crude materials for further processing; intermediate materials, supplies, and components; and finished goods. The finished goods index is the one usually picked up and reported in the press. In this index, consumer goods represent about 76 percent of the weight of the total index (27 percentage points are foods) and capital equipment 24 percent of the total. In addition to the three basic indexes, separate computations are made for prices at various stages of processing excluding food and energy components.

Not surprisingly, the producer price indexes are more volatile than either the CPI or the GNP implicit price deflator. Figure 3.5 compares the year-to-year fluctuations in these three indexes for the period 1950 to 1990. As indicated in the figure, the dotted line representing the producer price index is the most volatile, followed by the consumer price index.

WHICH INDEX IS BEST?

As is the case in most indexes, no one index is "best"; it depends on what you want to measure. The GNP deflator is the broadest measure and best reflects the movements of prices in a dynamic economy. The fixed-weight index is the broadest measure of prices alone, but becomes less meaningful as you

Figure 3.5. CPI versus PPI versus GNP Deflator

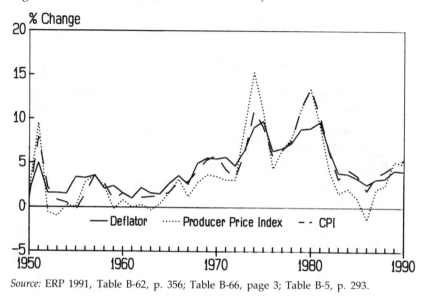

Source: ERP 1991, Table B-62, p. 356; Table B-66, page 3; Table B-5, p. 293.

get further away from the base year. The chain index is useful only for short-term comparisons. The defects in these indexes are that they are issued only quarterly and are subject to frequent revisions.

The CPI is a monthly index and is prepared by sampling, so that month-to-month revisions do not occur. However, the index becomes less meaningful as purchasing patterns change or quality improvements occur; that is, higher prices for better products. Revisions in the composition of the index are made only about every ten years, so they can get out of date in reflecting buying patterns of the consumer.

The CPI also differs from the price indexes for personal consumption expenditures in the GNP accounts. The CPI represents prices of a fixed-market basket of goods, reflecting the purchases in various geographical areas in a certain base period. Personal consumption expenditure prices used in the GNP accounts are estimates of the prices of those amounts of goods and services taken off the market by all consumers in a particular quarter or year.

The producer price indexes are used more by economists as foreshadowing indicators of commodity prices that will later affect goods prices in the CPI. These indexes are also used by manufacturers to track prices of their products as well as their raw materials and intermediate components. Given the growing importance of services in the economy, measuring only goods prices has limited usefulness to the average consumer or investor.

SUMMARY

This chapter described the three price indexes that are issued as a part of the regular GNP reports: the implicit price deflator, the fixed-weight index, and the chain price index. In addition, the consumer price index and the producer price indexes were discussed. Although the CPI is probably the best known, no one index is "best"; it depends on what is being measured. For example, the fixed-weight index of the GNP is the broadest measure of just price changes in the economy.

CHAPTER 4

Tracking the Consumer

In this chapter the various components of GNP are discussed. In this and the next three chapters the various GNP components are reviewed in more detail, providing additional background and historical perspective. Several other economic reports, which are helpful in following the performance of a particular sector, are also discussed.

This chapter is about the consumer. Many of the statistics reported regularly in the financial press deal with consumer income, spending, and savings. Such emphasis is appropriate, because the consumer is one of the most important players on the economic scene. Personal income is significant because it is the source of both spending and savings in the economy. Personal consumption accounts for about two-thirds of GNP, and changes in consumer spending can have a significant effect on business conditions; personal savings are a significant portion of total savings in the economy.

A review of the regular statistical reports that economists track to follow the movement of consumer income, spending, and savings is provided in this chapter. Some of the reports that cover personal income are:

> *Personal income.* A monthly report that reflects the two sources of this income—current production (e.g., wages and salaries, other labor income, personal interest, dividend and rental income, partnership and proprietors income) and transfer payments from business and government to persons (e.g., payments from a corporate health plan or social security payments);

> *Monthly employment report.* Provides information on the sources of personal income. A sample survey of households gives information on the size of the labor force and data on employment and unemployment. A survey of payroll reports gives information on payroll employment; the change in jobs in service, manufacturing, and related industries; and weekly and hourly earnings.

Personal spending by consumers is tracked by these reports:

> *Personal consumption expenditures.* Reported monthly, indicating consumer spending for durable goods, nondurable goods, and services;

> *Automobile sales.* Reported three times a month, the earliest and clearest indication of this important part of consumer durable spending;

Retail sales. Available monthly before the personal consumption report, reflecting spending for durable and nondurable goods. Because of the volatile nature of this report, it is difficult to interpret; other measures of consumer spending are more useful;

Housing starts and *building permits.* Reported monthly, indicating future trends in residential consumption expenditures.

Consumer savings and borrowing are measured as follows:

Personal savings. Reported monthly, a part of the income and expenditure report and essentially the difference between income and spending. However, personal savings are only a part of total sources of savings. Undistributed corporate profits, depreciation, state and local government surpluses, and funds from abroad are also included in the total sources of savings;

Consumer borrowing. Available monthly, measured by consumer installment data. However, month-to-month changes of credit outstanding or credit related to income are of little assistance in short-term business analysis.

Another way to follow whether the consumer will spend or save is to ask about consumer attitudes toward the economy and plans for the future.

Consumer attitudes. Tracked by sample surveys that ask questions of consumers about general business conditions, job availability, and buying intentions.

PERSONAL INCOME

Trends in personal income foreshadow changes in spending. In Table 2.3, the income side of GNP is described, moving from GNP to national income and then the distribution of this income among production costs and profits. Recall that the components of national income are:

Employee compensation, including wages and salaries, and employer contributions to employee benefit funds;

Net interest received by business;

Corporate profits;

Rental income of persons;

Income of proprietorships and partnerships.

If corporate profits and net interest received by business are subtracted from national income, the remainder is income from current production that goes to persons. However, a few other adjustments must be made in order to get to personal income. These are shown in Table 4.1, which shows the full relationship between national income and personal income.

Table 4.1.
Relationship of National Income and Personal Income—1990

National Income	$4,418.2
Subtract: Corporate Profits	298.7
Net Interest Received by Business	466.6
Contributions for Social Insurance	506.9
Add: Personal Interest Income	680.7
Personal Dividend Income	123.8
Business Transfer Payments	35.0
Government Transfer Payments to Persons	659.6
Personal Income	$4,645.1

Personal income is derived from two sources—income from current production, and transfer payments from business and government. As the table indicates, one way of estimating personal income is to start with national income and subtract those payments not made to persons—corporate profits, net interest received by business, and the contributions both business and individuals make to the government for social insurance. Contributions to social insurance are subtracted because this amount represents income *earned* in any particular period (and thus is a part of national income) but not actually *received*.

Certain transfers made from business and government to individuals must then be added. These transfers include interest income and dividend income paid to individuals, and business transfer payments for such things as bad debts (the forgiveness of which is considered income to consumers). Government transfer payments include benefits such as social security payments, health benefits, unemployment insurance, veterans benefits, and retirement benefits for government employees.

Figure 4.1 indicates the significance of each of the components of personal income to the total; the data are for the calendar year 1990. Wages and salaries are the largest component, accounting for 58 percent of total personal income. Another 6 percent is accounted for by other labor income, consisting of employer payments to private pension funds and welfare funds, such as health and life insurance and workers' compensation. Personal interest income is the second largest component at 14 percent, and transfer payments from business and government is third at 10 percent. Proprietors and partnership income accounts for 9 percent; dividends paid to persons accounts for 3 percent. Rental income received by persons accounts for less than 1 percent of personal income.

The Department of Commerce releases data on personal income in the third or fourth week of each month to cover the

Figure 4.1. Personal Income—1990

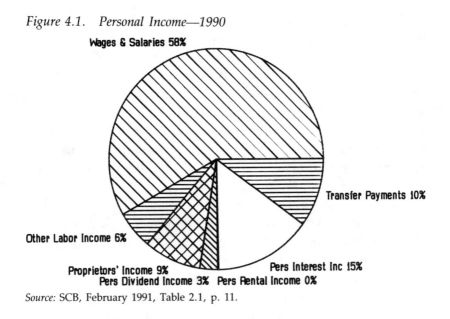

Source: SCB, February 1991, Table 2.1, p. 11.

information for the prior month. Personal income data are also included as a part of the monthly reports provided by the Commerce Department on the quarterly movements in GNP.

Monthly Employment Report

Because the monthly income report comes out late in the following month, another economic report issued earlier in the month is examined more closely; it provides the first indication of future changes in personal income. The monthly employment report covers the employment and unemployment situation, especially the part indicating the number of employees on nonagricultural payrolls. This information is released by the Bureau of Labor Statistics about the 5th of each month, covering information for the previous month.

Unfortunately, only part of the information in the monthly report is presented by the news media. Two key items are the percent of the labor force unemployed and the number of jobs created (or lost) in a particular month. However, the full significance of the report is not often discussed. Therefore, it is worthwhile to examine some of the background and the essential features of the monthly release.

The Household Survey. Two basic methods are used to assemble the data in the monthly employment report. The first method provides information on households and is gathered in a monthly survey of a sample of households scientifically designed to represent the civilian noninstitutional population. Inmates of institutions and persons under 16 years of age are excluded when computing the employment and unemployment statistics. Data on members of the armed forces in the United States are obtained from the Department of Defense and added to the estimate of the civilian labor force to obtain the size of the total labor force.

Each month about 55,800 households are visited for an interview; three-quarters of the household sample is common from one month to the next and half of the sample is common with the same month a year ago. The purpose of the interviews is to obtain information about the employment status of each member of the household 16 years of age and older.

In the household surveys, employed persons are those who, during the survey week (the week that includes the 12th of the month), worked as paid employees or in their own business, or who are not working but were temporarily absent from their jobs because of illness, bad weather, vacation, labor-management disputes, or personal reasons. Unemployed persons are those who were available for work, and had made specific efforts to find employment some time during the prior four weeks but had no employment during the survey week. (This definition is especially significant when comparing the unemployment rate in the United States with that of other countries, where unemployment is defined as a person actually collecting unemployment insurance.)

From the surveys and the information from the Department of Defense, the following data are computed:

Size of the civilian and the total labor force;

Number of persons employed and unemployed;

Duration of unemployment;

Number of job seekers;

Unemployment rates by various categories, such as sex, race, and age.

The Establishment Data.   The second source of employment information is based on payroll reports that provide current information on wage and salary employment as well as hours and earnings in individual nonagricultural establishments, categorized by industry and geographic location. Employment data refer to persons on payrolls who receive pay for any part of the pay period that includes the 12th of the month. Excluded are people who are on layoff, on leave without pay, or on strike during the entire period.

The number of establishments included in the report varies by industry. In order to ensure adequate coverage, more establishments are covered in industries with smaller size establishments. About 250,000 establishments are covered each month, which employ about one-third of total workers in the United States.

The information in the establishment reports permits computation of:

Number of people on payrolls for production and related workers in manufacturing and mining;

Construction workers in construction;

Nonsupervisory employees in private service-producing industries.

Other information provided includes:

Increase or decreases in jobs in service, manufacturing, and related industries;

Average weekly hours per employee;

Average hourly earnings;

Average weekly earnings.

From all of this information, economists pay the most attention to the total change in employees on nonagricultural payrolls. The data for the months in 1987 to 1990 are shown in Figure 4.2. Monthly changes are indicated by the dotted line on the figure. Monthly changes fluctuate widely; to smooth the data and make it easier to interpret, a three-month moving average of monthly changes has been computed, shown by the solid black line. One further adjustment has been to remove from the data the number of census workers that were added to the labor force between January and May 1990 and then subsequently eliminated from June through the end of the year. Their inclusion would make the numbers even more volatile and would not reveal underlying trends of employment.

A review of the figure indicates the importance of several years of data. Beginning in 1989, job increases definitely shifted to a level lower than that of the previous two years, and the significant drop in job gains in 1990 is evident. This perspective provided early indications of a definite slowing in the U.S. economy in the latter part of 1990.

Figure 4.2.   Change in Employees on Nonaq Payrolls

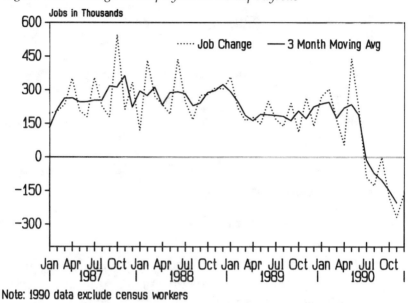

Note: 1990 data exclude census workers

Source: SCB, February 1991, p. S-10; data prior to December 1989 obtained directly from BLS.

Unfortunately, the monthly information on changes in payroll employment is often revised and the revisions may seem large. However, the changes are a very small percent of the total number of jobs. For example, a monthly change of as much as 100,000 jobs is a change of less than 0.1 percent on a job base of 108 million. When reviewing job changes, the initial report should be viewed with some degree of skepticism until revised data are reported in the next two months.

Other Employment and Unemployment Data.   The number that gets the most attention in the media is the monthly unemployment rate, probably because of its political sensitivity. Not surprisingly, unemployment rises in business-cycle contractions and falls in business expansions. However, *some* unemployment is inevitable, so-called frictional unemployment caused by people changing jobs, moving from one place to another, deciding to enter the labor force when another member of the family becomes unemployed, and so on. An acceptable level of frictional unemployment is more of a political than an economic issue. However, most economists would now accept the idea that rates much below 5 to 5½ percent for all practical purposes represent "full" employment in the United States.

A problem in interpreting the unemployment rate is the difficulty in measuring unemployment in the summer months, with the entry and exit of many students into and out of the labor force. Attempts are made to adjust for this seasonal phenomenon, but the number of summer job seekers varies so much from year to year that unusual variations in the unemployment rate during these months should be expected.

The monthly employment report does contain some helpful bits of information. The employment report is a good indicator of the change that will occur in the monthly industrial production index reported by the Federal Reserve about the 15th of each month. Many of the components of the industrial production index are estimated based on man-hour production data rather than the output of physical units. An increase in payroll employment and hours worked usually indicates an increase in industrial production.

Another helpful bit of information in the monthly employment report is contained in the average hourly earnings data. By comparing month-to-month or year-to-year changes over a period of time, some feeling of the rate of change in wages can be obtained. As seen in Table 2.3, wages are a very important component of production costs. Wages rising faster than prices foreshadows future price increases. As indicated in Figure 3.1, changes in consumer prices, excluding food and energy and changes in compensation, have tracked each other rather well.

PERSONAL CONSUMPTION EXPENDITURES

A report on *personal consumption expenditures* (PCE) accompanies the monthly report of personal income. Plotting these two series in a figure would result in two lines that move steadily upward. Therefore, as in the case of nonagricultural payroll employment, the month-to-month changes have been plotted instead. Figure 4.3 plots these changes in monthly personal income and personal consumption expenditures from 1987 to 1990.

As the figure shows, the lines move up and down erratically, making it hard to discern underlying trends. However, a downward trend is evident in 1990 in gains in personal income, which ultimately should result in a reduction in consumer spending.

Figure 4.3.   % Change in Personal Income and Expenditures

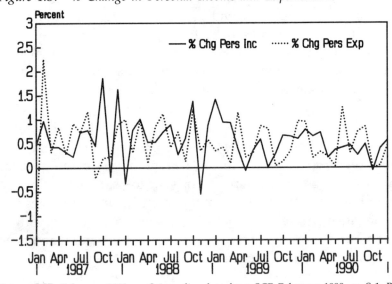

Source: SCB, February 1991, p. S-1; earlier data from SCB February 1990, p. S-1; BS, p. 1–2.

This information is useful in following trends over a period of months. However, the availability of the data late in the month makes it a less useful indicator of current business conditions. The wealth of detail in the report is more useful to analysts of particular areas of the economy. Some of this detail is discussed below.

Personal consumption expenditures are divided into durable goods (goods expected to last three years or more), nondurable goods, and services. Figure 4.4. compares PCE in 1950 with those in 1990. In viewing the two circles, keep in mind that PCE increased about 19 times during this period; GNP increased slightly less.

Of more interest is the shifting composition of PCE. Durable goods purchases remained about constant: 16 percent of PCE in 1950 and 13 percent in 1990. However, nondurable goods purchases decreased from 51 to 33 percent, while services spending grew from 33 to 54 percent.

The shifts within the components are also interesting. Figure 4.5 indicates the shift in durable goods spending. Over

Figure 4.4. Personal Consumption Expenditures

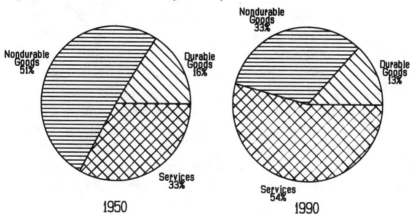

Source: 1990 data from SCB, February 1991, Table 1.1, p. 7; 1950 data from NIPA, Table 1.1, p. 7.

Figure 4.5.   PCE—Durables

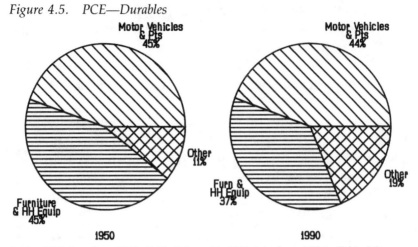

Source: 1990 data from SCB, Table 2.2, p. 11; 1950 data from NIPA, Table 2.2, p. 99.

the 1950 to 1990 period, durable spending increased about 15.6 times, less than the increase in total PCE. Within durable goods spending, motor vehicles and parts remained the largest area of spending at about 45 percent. The shrinkage occurred in furniture and household equipment; purchases shifted to durable spending on other items, including sports equipment, boats, durable toys, jewelry, and watches.

Figure 4.6 shows the changes in spending for nondurables. Total spending for nondurables grew about 12 times during the 1950 to 1990 period. Most of the large components of spending decreased during this period: food from 55 to 52 percent; clothing from 20 to 18 percent; fuel oil and coal from 3 to 2 percent. Gasoline and oil spending rose slightly from 6 to 8 percent. The decreases reflected increased "other" spending for nondurables, including toilet articles, drug preparations, semidurable house furnishings, nondurable toys, and sport supplies.

Figure 4.7 indicates the shift in PCE for services. This segment increased more than 31 times from 1950 to 1990, com-

Figure 4.6. PCE—Nondurables

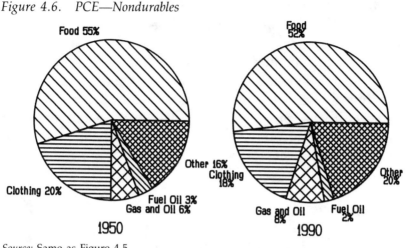

1950 | 1990

Source: Same as Figure 4.5

pared to a rise in GNP of 19 times. The change in the composition of services spending is even more interesting. The percent of service expenditures for housing, household operations, and transportation decreased slightly, but the percent of service expenditures for medical care expanded dramatically—an increase of more than 70 times during this period! "Other" ex-

Figure 4.7. PCE—Services

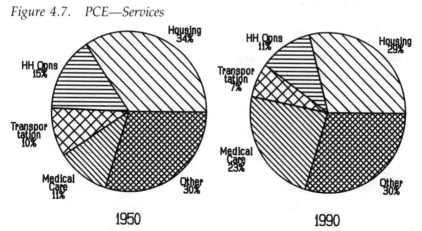

1950 | 1990

Source: Same as Figure 4.5

penditures held their percent of the total; these expenditures included items such as personal care, recreation, personal business costs, religious and welfare activities, and private education. Services spending fluctuates less in business cycles than spending for durables. The increased portion of consumer spending for services, especially for such important items as medical care, has provided greater stability to overall consumer spending. This greater stability has tempered the severity of business downturns.

AUTOMOBILE SALES

Although the smallest of the three areas of consumer spending, the series watched most carefully is spending for durables, because purchase of these items are postponable and therefore fluctuate cyclically. Almost half of durable spending is for automobiles and parts. Because of its importance in both the cyclical part of personal spending and the automobile industry in the economy as a whole, automobile sales are a carefully watched statistic that reflects the spending mood of the consumer and indicates possible future increases or decreases in production.

Information on automobile sales has two major advantages relative to other economic information. In the first place, they are available early; sales are reported for three relatively equal monthly segments, with the information available five business days after the 10th, 20th, and last day of the month. Second, unlike many statistics, the numbers are not subject to later revisions, so that the first report can be relied on as accurate.

One caution should be kept in mind in interpreting the data. Ten-day sales are often reported in the news media compared with sales for the similar period of the previous year—

hardly significant when dealing with a time period as short as ten days. In addition to the ten-day sales results, the news media also may report the seasonally adjusted annual rate of sales for domestically produced cars, a computation prepared by the Department of Commerce. Even with seasonally adjusted data, however, one ten-day period is not especially meaningful.

One way of tracking automobile sales is shown in Figure 4.8. Domestic sales are shown monthly at seasonally adjusted annual rates, with the current year plotted against sales for the two previous years. Seasonally adjusted sales of imported cars are also plotted, although this information is not ordinarily published in the financial press. However, it can be found each month in the Commerce Department's publication *Survey of*

Figure 4.8.   Automobile Sales—Domestic and Imports

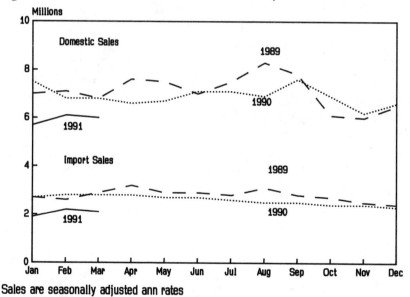

Sales are seasonally adjusted ann rates

Source: SCB, February 1991, p. S-32; earlier issues of SCB for data prior to December 1989.

Current Business. It is shown here to indicate that these sales generally follow the pattern of domestic car sales; consequently, for short-term business analysis, sales of domestic cars can be used. Using data plotted monthly, each ten-day sales figure can be noted in the figure, with the final plot for the month made when the monthly data are available.

The weakness in domestic automobile sales in the last part of 1990 and early 1991 stands out very clearly in the figure. In the fall of 1989, sales of new 1990 models were initially weak because manufacturers discontinued sales incentives. When they were reinstated, sales increased by year's end. In the fall of 1990 and in early 1991, however, sales of new 1991 models slumped in spite of sales incentives, indicating contracting consumer spending for durables.

RETAIL SALES

Another report available about midmonth—and therefore available before the report on personal consumption—is retail sales. These sales are accounted for by a broad variety of stores, as illustrated in Figure 4.9. About 36 percent of retail sales are accounted for by sales of durable goods, which is shown by the three separated slices of the pie chart. Auto and parts stores account for 24 percent of total retail sales and about two-thirds of durable goods sales by retail stores. Because durable goods sales are more volatile than total retail sales, and auto and parts are such a significant part of durable goods sales, fluctuations in domestic auto sales figures can provide a good clue to the subsequent retail sales number. Food store sales represent about 22 percent of retail sales; eating and drinking establishments another 11 percent. Department stores, more accurately described as general merchandising stores, account for just 13 percent of total retail sales. Thus, when the news media report

Figure 4.9. Retail Sales—1989

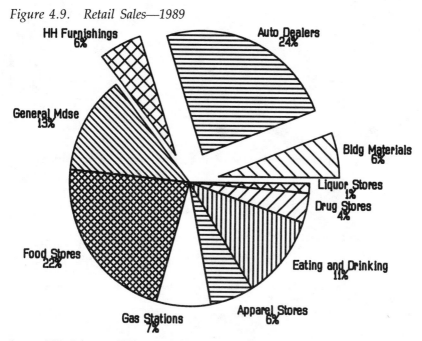

HH Furnishings
6%

Auto Dealers
24%

General Mdse
13%

Bldg Materials
6%

Liquor Stores
1%

Drug Stores
4%

Food Stores
22%

Eating and Drinking
11%

Gas Stations
7%

Apparel Stores
6%

Source: SCB, February 1991, pps. 8–9.

the sales results of the major retail stores about a week before retail sales are available, the report is not necessarily a good indicator of total retail trade.

The pattern of monthly change in retail sales is illustrated on Figure 4.10, which plots this information for the months of 1987 to 1990. As the figure illustrates, the monthly changes are erratic, so that drawing conclusions from one or two month's data is hardly warranted.

Figure 4.11 plots the two components of retail sales for the period 1987 to 1990: durables and nondurables. The principal conclusion that can be drawn from this figure is that durable sales are more volatile than nondurable sales. In fact, the latter generally have positive changes (as shown by movements above the zero line). Nondurable sales generally increase each

Figure 4.10.   Retail Sales—Monthly Percent Change

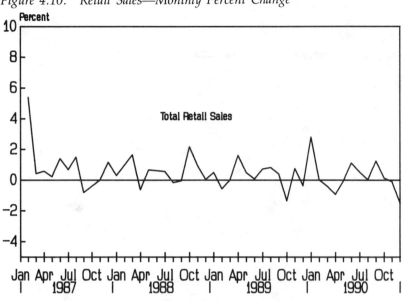

Source; SCB, February 1991, p. S-8; earlier data direct from Bureau of Census.

Figure 4.11.   Retail Sales—Monthly Percent Change Durables and Nondurables

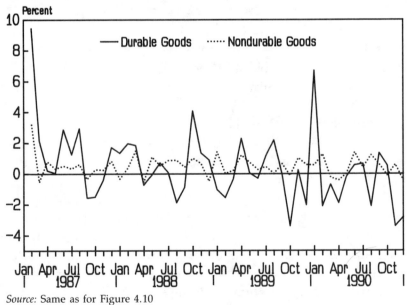

Source: Same as for Figure 4.10

month; durables sales are much more erratic. The difficulties in interpreting monthly retail sales figures favor using automobile sales and consumer confidence measures as better indicators of near-term consumer spending trends.

CONSTRUCTION

Other monthly statistics that reflect large consumer commitments are the reports on the dollar value of residential construction as well as housing starts and permits, especially for single-family units. Total construction expenditures, exceeding $400 billion a year, are of considerable economic significance. Private construction accounts for about 80 percent of total construction expenditures; public construction accounts for the other 20 percent. New residential construction accounts for more than 40 percent of private construction.

The dollar value of construction and its components are available about two months after the reported month. For example, October data are reported in early December. However, it is not especially useful in evaluating the current economic scene because it is one of the late statistics available, and is often revised.

Residential investment is also reported as a part of the quarterly GNP accounts. One of the components of GNP is fixed investment, which includes private residential as well as nonresidential investment. (Government investment is included in government purchases of goods and services in the GNP accounts.) Nonresidential investment will be discussed in Chapter 5, which is devoted to the business sector.

Residential investment in the GNP accounts is divided into single-family homes (about half of total residential investment), multifamily homes (10 percent); the remainder is accounted for by additions and alterations, mobile homes, hotels, dormitories, nursing homes, and brokerage commissions on sales. Residential construction is one of the more volatile areas of investment. It averaged 4.7 percent of GNP in the past 30 years, ranging from a low of 3.3 percent in 1982 to a high of 5.7 percent in 1972 and 1978. Because the data on residential investment in the GNP accounts is available only quarterly and is usually revised, it is not given as much attention in the analysis of current business conditions as other monthly series that report on residential construction.

Residential construction is usually tracked by monthly data on housing starts, divided into single- and multifamily units. Each single-family house and each separate apartment within an apartment building are counted as one housing start. The measure includes both privately and publicly owned housing. Data are collected by the Census Bureau and are available during the third week of the month following the reported month. The data are seasonally adjusted and reported at annual rates.

Another series reported at the same time is building permits, or new construction authorizations currently granted to builders by local government bodies. The Bureau of the Census obtains the data by a mail survey of local building permit officials. The permit data account for almost 90 percent of total housing starts. The relationship between permits and starts may not be too close, because the time between obtaining a permit and starting the house may vary.

Figure 4.12 provides a useful way of following starts and permits. The data are plotted monthly for the 1987 to 1990 period. Permit activity roughly leads starts, as seen in the figure. The near collapse of both permits and starts beginning in early 1990 is evident.

Residential investment decisions may initially be made by builders and contractors, but ultimately individuals make these decisions. Consequently, residential construction is affected by the growth in the number of households in the long term and

Figure 4.12. Housing Starts and Building Permits

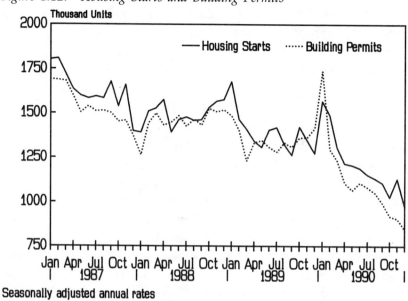

Seasonally adjusted annual rates

Source: ERP 1991, Table B-53, p. 346; data for 1987–88 from earlier ERP.

by mortgage interest rates and the growth of family income in the short term.

One factor to keep in mind in reviewing housing data is to remember that the data are at seasonally adjusted annual rates. Because housing is affected significantly by weather, few starts are actually made in many sections of the country in the winter months. Should winter weather be unusually mild, a small increase in the actual unadjusted number of housing starts can be translated into a big surge when the figures are seasonally adjusted—a factor clearly evident in the winter of 1989 to 1990.

CONSUMER SAVINGS

In addition to a current income stream, the consumer can obtain funds for consumption from either past savings or borrowing. Month-to-month changes in these two factors are not especially significant in determining future consumer spending, but trends over several years in the savings rate and borrowing can be informative. This section discusses consumer savings; borrowing is discussed in the next section.

Information on the *consumer savings rate* is available monthly as a part of the report on personal income and spending; it is also available monthly as a part of the estimates contained in the quarterly national income and product account release. Table 4.2 shows the relationship between personal income and personal savings.

As the consumer becomes more concerned about the future, savings are likely to increase; the opposite is also true. However, this measure is not very precise. As Table 4.2 illustrates, savings are a residual derived by subtracting estimated personal consumption and personal tax payments from personal income, and as a residual, it reflects all of the errors (some of them offsetting) in the figures used to derive it.

In addition, large segments of consumer spending are estimates rather than calculated directly. For example, in the case of owner-occupied homes, an estimate is made of the rental value of the dwellings less all of the costs associated with owning the dwelling, including mortgage interest. The personal savings figure does not take into account the effects of capital gains and losses, such as an increase or decrease in the value of

Table 4.2.
Personal Income and Personal Savings—1990 (Billions of Dollars)

Personal Income	$4,645.1
Less: Personal Tax and Nontax Payments	699.4
Equals: Disposable Personal Income	3,945.6
Less: Personal Consumption Expenditures	3,658.6
Interest Paid by Consumers to Business	107.8
Personal Transfer Payments to Foreigners	0.9
Equals: Personal Savings	178.4
Personal Savings as a Percent of Disposable Personal Income: 4.5%	

residential real estate or the decrease in the value of stock holdings after a sharp market rise or drop. It also does not reflect the creation of financial credit by the banking system and the Federal Reserve, which can expand consumer purchasing power. Consequently, small monthly shifts in the savings number should not be given too much weight, although a trend downward or upward over a year or more is of considerable significance.

Even though these measures are imprecise, why is tracking savings important? For individuals, savings are important because some funds should be set aside for family emergencies or for longer term family objectives. For the country as a whole, savings are viewed differently, as indicated in the following relationships:

Total *output* of the economy generates *income* equal to the value of that output;

And *income* minus *consumption* equals *savings*;

But *output* minus *consumption* equals *investment*;

Consequently, *savings* equals *investment*.

The larger the savings in a society the greater the sum available for investment. The greater the investment, the greater the potential for productivity gains of its work force, leading to a more prosperous country as a whole. Consequently, following the long-term trends of savings measures can provide useful clues to the future performance of the economy.

Figure 4.13 plots the annual personal savings rate in the United States for the years 1950 to 1990. For 1950 to 1990, this savings rate averaged 6.7 percent of disposable personal income. It reached a postwar peak of 9.4 percent in 1973, fell to a low point of 2.9 percent in 1987, and in 1989 rose to 4.6 percent. It fell slightly to 4.5 percent in 1990. In spite of the imperfec-

Figure 4.13.   Personal Savings Rate

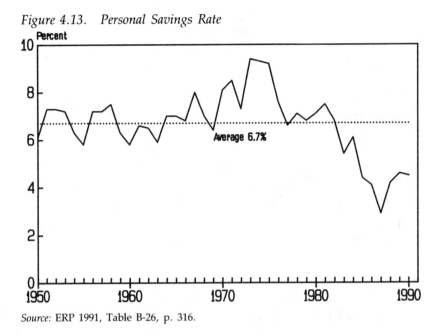

Source: ERP 1991, Table B-26, p. 316.

tions of the data, the below-average performance since 1985 has been a cause of concern about sluggish personal savings.

Other Savings Measures

Personal savings can be measured in other ways. The Federal Reserve, for example, prepares a quarterly estimate of personal savings that includes as a part of savings consumer durable goods purchases, government insurance credits, and capital gains. This savings rate has also trended downward since the mid-1970s, but in 1990 it was 10.6 percent, more than twice the Commerce estimate of the savings rate.

The savings estimates mentioned thus far are measures of only personal savings. Undistributed profits of corporate business as well as depreciation credits of corporate and noncorporate business are a form of savings and should be included when estimating savings. State and local governments have been running an annual surplus of funds in excess of expenditures, which adds to the savings stream; and of increasing importance to the United States is the net flow of funds from abroad.

Savings are used for business fixed investments, residential investment, and increases in business inventories. Another significant user of savings is the federal government, which has been running an annual deficit. Table 4.3 summarizes these sources and uses of savings in the United States for the year 1990. The total savings in 1990 represented about 17 percent of GNP, close to the average of about 18 percent in recent years.

As indicated in Table 4.3, personal savings in 1990 accounted for under 20 percent of total savings. The largest source of savings is business depreciation allowances (approximately 63 percent) and, when added to undistributed corporate profits, accounts for two-thirds of savings. Savings in the

Table 4.3.
Sources and Uses of Savings—1990

	Billions of Dollars	Percent
Sources of Savings		
Personal Savings (Commerce Definition)	$178.4	19.6
Undistributed Corporate Profits	29.8	3.3
Depreciation, Corporate, and Noncorporate	575.7	63.3
State and Local Government Surpluses	36.2	4.0
Net Foreign	88.8	9.8
Total	$908.9	100.0
Uses of Savings		
Nonresidential Fixed Investment	$523.7	57.6
Residential Construction	222.4	24.5
Decreases in Business Inventories	− 4.2	−0.5
Federal Deficit	163.9	18.0
Statistical Discrepancy	3.1	0.4
Total	$908.9	100.0

business sector were larger than use of savings by business for plant, equipment, and inventories. Personal savings were not large enough to take care of the demand for residential construction. State and local surpluses and funds from abroad were not sufficient to cover the federal deficit; it also claimed savings from the private sector. Had the funds from abroad not been so large, funding the federal deficit would have absorbed even more of domestic savings, further reducing the amount available to the private sector and forcing interest rates up. To put it another way, lower federal deficits would have released funds that could have been used for business investment to improve productivity and create new jobs.

CONSUMER BORROWING

Information about consumer borrowing is provided monthly by the Federal Reserve Board about six weeks after the month to which the data refer. This series on consumer installment credit covers most short- to intermediate-term credit extended to individuals scheduled to be repaid in two or more installments. The major categories of credit are automobile credit (about 40 percent of the total), and revolving credit, for example, credit cars and check credit plans (about 28 percent). Other loans, such as mobile homes, home improvement, vans and pickup trucks, and student loans, are reported in an additional category. The figures represent the amount outstanding at the end of each month and reflect the net effect of extensions and repayments.

Figure 4.14 shows consumer installment as a percent of personal income for the years 1950 to 1990. The broad upsweep of credit relative to income is evident through the mid-1960s, when it leveled off. A sharp reduction occurred during the business contractions in 1980 and 1981, but then the percentage rose rapidly, reaching record heights in 1989. Outstanding

Figure 4.14.   Consumer Installment Credit as Percent Personal Income

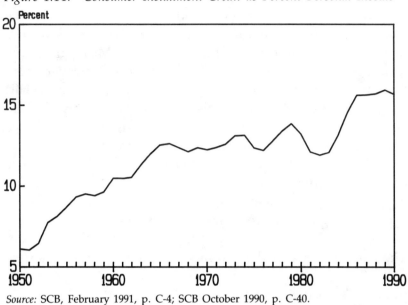

Source: SCB, February 1991, p. C-4; SCB October 1990, p. C-40.

consumer credit typically expands and contracts as the economy expands and contracts, so that it accentuates the cyclical
nature of consumer spending, especially for durables. Consumer borrowing is now near record levels; this high debt
position of the consumer may intensify the severity of the next
business contraction. However, because the data are released
late and because the month-to-month changes are of limited
significance, the consumer credit data are not critical for short-
term business analysis.

CONSUMER ATTITUDES

Two other sources of information on the consumer are
surveys of consumer attitudes, compiled by The Conference
Board, a nonprofit private research organization in New York,
and the Survey Research Center of the University of Michigan

in Ann Arbor. The Conference Board survey results are available in the first week of the month for the survey taken the prior month; the results usually are reported in the financial press, especially in the *Wall Street Journal*. The Michigan survey results are made available only to subscribers. However, summary indexes of both surveys are reported in tabular and chart form by the Department of Commerce in its monthly publication *Survey of Current Business*. Unfortunately, the survey data are several months old by the time the *Survey* is published.

The Conference Board consumer confidence index reflects consumer attitudes about the general business situation and job availability. The Board also publishes an index of consumer expectations, in which consumers express their opinions on the outlook for business, jobs, and their own financial situation. The data are converted to an index (with 1985 used as a base

Figure 4.15.   Consumer Confidence and Expectations

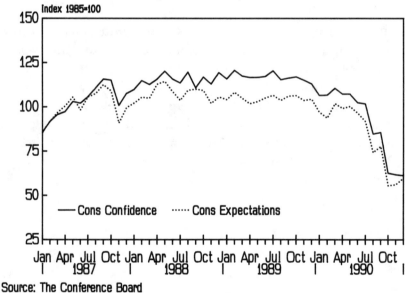

Source: The Conference Board

Source: SCB, February 1991, p. C-2; earlier data direct from Bureau of Economic Analysis, Department of Commerce.

index), but the significance is in the rise and fall of the index rather than any particular level. Figure 4.15 plots both the confidence and expectations indexes monthly from 1987–90. The downward drift in confidence that took place in early 1990 and the sharp drop in August that coincided with the Middle East crisis is clearly shown.

SUMMARY

Consumer spending accounts for the bulk of GNP. Consumer spending for durables, although the smallest percent of spending, is the most volatile and has the greatest cyclical significance. During the past 40 years, spending for services has risen from 33 to 53 percent of consumer spending, which has stabilized spending and lowered the cyclical vulnerability of the economy.

A wealth of data is available for analysis of the consumer sector. Some information is current, and movements in this information, for example, automobile sales, are very important in assessing the short-term outlook for the economy. Other information must be examined in a longer term perspective and is useful primarily in analyzing the condition of the economy, a condition that may persist for some time. In the following list those data most useful for short-term analysis are marked with an ''*''

Early in the month:

Automobile sales*;

The monthly employment report*;

The dollar value of construction for two months previous.

Midmonth:

> Automobile sales*;
>
> Retail sales*;
>
> Housing starts*;
>
> Consumer confidence index*;
>
> Consumer price index*;
>
> Consumer credit for two months previous.

Late in the month:

> Automobile sales*;
>
> Personal income and personal consumption expenditures;
>
> The savings rate.

Monitoring these reports—most importantly those marked—can provide meaningful information about this important sector of the economy.

CHAPTER 5

Following the Business Sector

This chapter initially considers those accounts of the GNP that deal with business investment: spending for plant and equipment, and additions to, or subtractions from, business inventories. The place of manufacturing in the economy and the statistics used to follow that sector will also be discussed.

Remember that the GNP accounts reflect only final demand, which is why personal consumption accounts for such a large part of GNP. Business activity is largely involved in producing or processing things, or providing services that will be consumed by others. As a result, the complex activities of business are not fully captured in the GNP accounts; only business investment is captured. Therefore, many other statistical series have to be reviewed to understand the contribution of business to the functioning of the economy.

The specific concepts considered in this chapter are:

Business capital investment, or *plant and equipment spending*. Used for further production;

Fixed investment. In the GNP accounts include *private residential* and *nonresidential* investment. Nonresidential investment is divided into *structures* and *producers durable equipment*. Residential investment is discussed in Chapter 4;

Surveys of business spending; actual and planned, as well as *new orders for nondefense capital goods*. Useful predictors of future business spending plans. Other helpful measures are the monthly report on *capacity utilization* and quarterly information on *corporate cash flow*;

Changes in business inventories. Important causes of business cycles. Inventory changes are a part of the GNP accounts and *business sales and inventories* are reported on a monthly basis;

Industrial production. Reported monthly, an important measure of manufacturing activity. Other early indicators of manufacturing are the monthly reports of the *purchasing managers' index of activity* and *new orders for durable goods*.

BUSINESS CAPITAL INVESTMENT

An important part of business activity is *capital investment*, or investment in the plant and equipment that will be used for further production. Although not a large percent of GNP, investment in capital goods is one of the critical forces influencing the growth and well-being of the economy. Capital goods production generates wages, adding to the demand for consumer goods, leading to more wages seeking more consumer goods, and so on. Capital goods output therefore has a multiplier effect on economic expansion.

Plant and equipment investment also affects productivity, or output per hour of goods and services, and thus the long-term growth rate at which the economy can expand. Moreover, investment in plant and equipment is made in large amounts. It usually bulges toward the end of a business expansion as output approaches capacity limits. Therefore, plant and equipment investment is a critical factor in determining the magnitude of the fluctuations and the duration of business cycles.[1]

Total *fixed investment* averaged about 15 percent of GNP during the past four decades, ranging from as low as 14 percent of GNP in 1961 to a high of 17.6 percent in 1979. Fixed investment is divided into *private residential* and *nonresidential* investment. It does not include government investment, which is considered government purchases of goods and services in the GNP accounts. Residential investment (discussed in Chapter 4), accounts for about one-third of total fixed investment; nonresidential investment accounts for the remainder. Nonresidential investment is divided into *structures*, about one-third of nonresidential investment, and *producers durable equipment* (*PDE*), the remaining two-thirds. PDE essentially is the machines and equipment illustrated in Figure 5.2.

[1]Many people might consider purchases of consumer durable goods such as automobiles, furniture, and appliances as investment. However, by convention such purchases are treated in the national accounts as consumption rather than investment. These durable goods purchases were discussed in greater detail in Chapter 4.

Nonresidential Fixed Investment

Figure 5.1 plots total nonresidential fixed investment and its components as a percent of GNP for 1950 to 1990. The volatile nature of nonresidential fixed investment is evident. The rate of growth of GNP itself varies over time. Therefore, the changing percent of GNP accounted for by investment indicates that its volatility is greater than that of GNP. The other interesting factor is the rising trend in the percent of investment represented by PDE and the shrinking percent accounted for by structures. Buildings have become less important than what goes into them.

A clearer illustration of this divergence is shown in Figure 5.2, which compares the distribution of nonresidential fixed investment in 1950 with that in 1990. As the figure indicates, structures as a percent of the total decreased from 36 to 28

Figure 5.1.   Nonresidential Fixed Investment as a Percent GNP

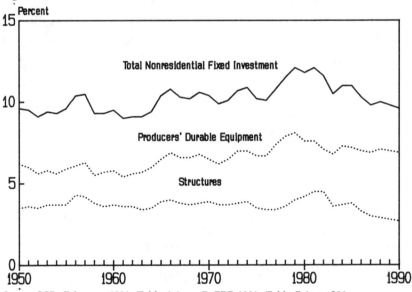

Source: SCB, February 1991, Table 1.1, p. 7; ERP 1991, Table B-1, p. 286.

Figure 5.2.   Nonresidential Fixed Investment Distribution

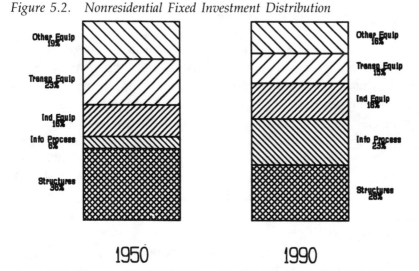

Source: SCB, February 1991, Table 5.12, p. 16; 1950 data NIPA, Table 5.5, 5.6, p. 231, 233.

percent. The biggest gain was in information processing equipment (office, computing, and accounting machinery; communication equipment; instruments; and photocopy and related equipment), which rose from 6 to 23 percent. As you might guess, photocopy equipment gained much more than the other three categories!

BUSINESS INVESTMENT EXPECTATIONS

The broadest series tracking business investment is the component of GNP called nonresidential fixed investment, which is reported as a part of the data in the monthly reports on quarterly GNP. These data, like all GNP components, are reported in current dollars and constant dollars; but other series are more useful in anticipating future movements in business fixed investment.

Surveys of Business Spending

Several other series released by the government can be used to anticipate future business investment spending reported in the GNP accounts. In April, June, September, and December, the Bureau of Census of the Department of Commerce publishes the results of a survey of historical and projected outlays for plant and equipment expenditures by U.S. business. The December figures project spending for the full calendar year ahead. The remaining reports combine actual and projected spending by quarters for the year. The data are shown in current and constant dollars and contain considerable industry detail. The survey is based on a sample of about 132,000 businesses that account for about 54 percent of all capital spending in the United States.

The information in this report differs from the information used in the GNP accounts for this sector; the survey report is based on information from the *users* of capital equipment, while the GNP data reflect information from *producers* of capital equipment. Various studies of the reliability of the projections indicate that the annual projections are more reliable than the quarterly estimates. A weakness of this survey can be the failure of companies to respond to the inquiries or the lack of attention within a company to ensure the accuracy of the reports. Nevertheless, the report is a helpful indicator of the general direction of spending, and reviewing successive reports can provide indications of weakening or strengthening in spending plans.

Nondefense Capital Goods Orders

A monthly series used to track present and future business investment is new orders, shipments, and unfilled orders (backlogs) for nondefense capital goods. This information is part of the monthly report on total manufacturers' new orders,

sales, inventories, and backlogs. Nondefense capital goods orders must be evaluated carefully—from time to time they can
be distorted by aircraft orders, which can be very large and
very volatile dollar items.

Figure 5.3 shows the pattern of new orders and shipments
for nondefense capital goods by month from January 1987
through 1990. The volatile nature of new orders is clearly evident, especially in the early months of 1990, due primarily to
big aircraft new orders in certain months. In spite of this volatility, a flattening trend in the new order series is evident in
late 1988 through 1990. The shipment pattern is much smooth-
er. New orders generally exceeding shipments indicate that
backlogs are increasing.

Another way of analyzing the nondefense capital goods
series is to follow the pattern of two key ratios shown in Figure
5.4: inventories to shipments and unfilled orders to shipments.
The first series indicates whether an inventory overhang of

Figure 5.3. Nondefense Capital Goods—New Orders and Shipments

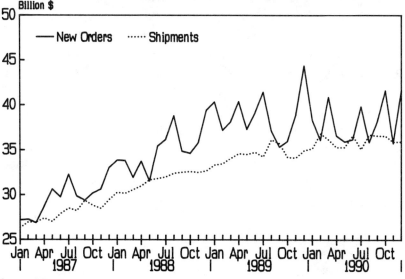

Source: SCB, February 1991, p. S-4. SCB earlier issues for earlier data.

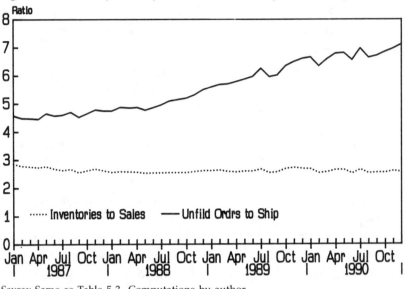

Figure 5.4.   Nondefense Capital Goods—Inventory and Backlog Ratios

Source: Same as Table 5.3. Computations by author.

capital goods is building up, which may be a problem requiring subsequent liquidation. The lower line of the figure indicates that this ratio has been fairly steady, so that at year end, 1990 capital goods inventories did not appear excessive.

The second series, the ratio of unfilled orders to shipments, indicates how many months of shipments at the current rate would be necessary to eliminate the current backlog if no further new orders were received. As the top line of the figure indicates, this series moved upward for most of the period surveyed, and toward the end of 1990, backlogs were equal to about seven months' shipments. Toward the end of 1990, neither of these series suggested a near-term weakness in business fixed-investment spending.

Determinants of Business Investment

Business investment decisions are usually influenced by two factors:

The cost of capital; and

The expected return on investment.

The cost of capital, which is critical in determining the return on investment, in turn is influenced by:

The level of interest rates; and

Tax law changes.

Interest rates will be discussed in Chapter 8. With respect to tax law changes, Congress has from time to time changed tax laws to encourage business investment. One way is to reduce the corporate tax rate, which encourages investment by lowering the so-called hurdle rate, the rate of return below which capital investments are not considered profitable.[2]

Another method of encouraging investment is to permit accelerated depreciation of capital equipment. By increasing the dollar amount of depreciation of assets in any one year, more corporate income is exempt from taxes because depreciation is a deduction from income before computing corporate income taxes. Thus higher depreciation means more income exempt from taxes, lowering the effective tax rate. Although depreciation charges do not represent a cash outlay, reducing tax payments presumably makes available additional funds to the corporation that could be used for investment.

Measuring Capacity Utilization

In addition to watching tax law changes, an important influence on future business fixed investment is the relationship of output to capacity.

[2]This rate varies from company to company and from industry to industry, depending on such factors as cost of capital, risk, competition, tax rates, and so on.

Why is *capacity utilization* important? As demand increases, rising utilization rates may require use of less efficient plant and will increase labor costs due to overtime and second shifts. These rising costs can cause price increases. Prolonged high utilization rates lead to increased business spending for plant and equipment. Measures of capacity utilization are used as indicators of business cycle turning points. Finally, capacity utilization measures are useful in estimating war mobilization capabilities.

Some Definitions. Most of us have an intuitive feeling that capacity is the maximum physical output that a plant can produce—that feeling is correct if we are talking about an engineering or war mobilization concept. However, operating "flat out" cannot be continued indefinitely. It assumes that no shortages of labor and materials impede production, that higher production costs such as overtime are not considered, and that downtime for maintenance and repairs is minimized. The concept of capacity becomes more elusive when we consider not just an individual plant but expand the concept to the capacity of a firm, an industry, or an economic sector (for example, manufacturing).

A different approach to capacity considers cost of production. Economists use two cost concepts: average or unit cost and marginal cost. Average cost is obtained by dividing the total cost of production by the current level of output. Marginal cost is the additional cost a firm incurs in producing one more unit of output. As the rate of output increases, average cost initially falls as fixed or overhead costs are spread over more units of production. However, at some point the fixed costs begin to rise (e.g., as machinery or labor is used more intensively). At that point, the cost of producing one more unit, or marginal cost, exceeds average cost, and average costs begin to rise. Consequently, an economic concept of capacity is the point where average costs are lowest, that is, where marginal costs and average costs are equal. Beyond that point, average costs begin to increase and future plant investment must be considered because the output is not being produced at the most efficient rate. Some consideration of these factors underlies any corporation's answer to what its production capacity is.

How Is Capacity Utilization Measured? Two government agencies provide measures of capacity utilization. The first is an annual survey conducted by the Bureau of the Census; the second is prepared monthly by the Federal Reserve Board.

The Bureau of the Census' annual survey in the fourth quarter of each year covers about 9,000 manufacturing establishments in 450 manufacturing industries. This survey compares the market value of output with the market value of both preferred and practical operations. *Preferred* operations are defined as the production level the firm would prefer to maintain (presumably where profits are maximized), and probably is related to the economic concept of capacity just described. *Practical* operations are defined as the production level that could reasonably be attained using existing work schedules and machinery and equipment in place and is more related to the engineering or war mobilization concept. Two separate capacity utilization rates are prepared from this information: a preferred operating rate and a practical operating rate. By the definitions of the Census Bureau, the preferred level may equal, but may not exceed, practical capacity.

The Federal Reserve Board provides a monthly report on capacity utilization, or output divided by capacity. This series provides information on total industry capacity, divided into manufacturing, mining, and utility sectors. Although focus is on total operating rates, 50 manufacturing components, 18 mining components, and 2 utility components are also covered.

The Federal Reserve, itself conducts no surveys of capacity, or utilization. It uses data from surveys of utilization rates made by other organizations, such as the Bureau of the Census, McGraw-Hill Publishing Company, and various trade associations. Presumably, the survey respondent has some idea of practical capacity in mind; it is not defined precisely by these surveying organizations. Capacity can then be measured by dividing output by the utilization rate. (If the capacity utilization rate is equal to output divided by capacity, then capacity can be computed by dividing output by the utilization rate.)

The Federal Reserve, in its estimation of monthly capacity, starts with these survey results, checks them against production indexes, and estimates the industry additions to capital stock, industry estimates of physical capacity, and businesses' estimates of changes in capacity. The Federal Reserve then prepares estimates of monthly capacity levels. To obtain operating rates, the Federal Reserve's monthly production index for certain industries as well as total manufacturing, mining, and utility sectors are divided by the appropriate capacity indexes to get utilization rates.

Limitations of the Data. Several limitations of the data must be mentioned. The Census survey is only available annually, and inadequate funding has prevented a survey for late 1989. It is also computed on a plant basis and therefore does not take into account bottlenecks or problems at a company, industry, or sector level. It is based on a market value rather than a physical volume basis. In addition, the respondent may or may not be knowledgeable in interpreting the questions, or the answers may not be representative of the industry or sector because of nonresponse. Consistency over time is difficult to achieve. Trends over longer periods of time are more informative than month-to-month changes.

Figure 5.5 indicates the total industry operating rate for the 1987 to 1990 period, as reported by the Federal Reserve. In addition, the high of the index in 1980 of 87.3 percent (the peak

Figure 5.5. *Total Industry Capacity Utilization*

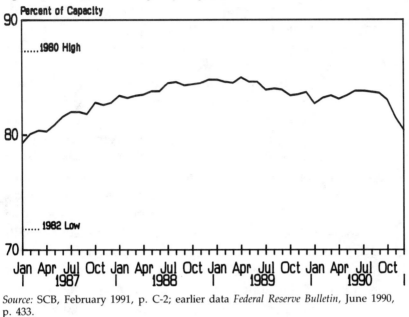

Source: SCB, February 1991, p. C-2; earlier data *Federal Reserve Bulletin*, June 1990, p. 433.

of the previous business cycle) and the 1982 low of 71.8 percent (the trough of the previous business cycle) are shown.

Typically, operating rates much above approximately 85 percent have signaled potential pressures on prices as more costly facilities are brought into production and factories move into overtime. The weakening of operating rates in the latter part of 1990 is evident, and these rates are heading still lower in early 1991.

CORPORATE CASH FLOW

In addition to operating rates as a foreshadowing indicator of business spending plans, *corporate cash flow* can also affect trends in spending. Cash flow consists of corporate profits after taxes plus depreciation. Depreciation allowances, as mentioned earlier, are a permitted business expense deducted before taxes; they are not cash outlays.

Cash flow is reported after two adjustments are made. The first excludes *inventory profits*, which are not considered coming from current production.[3] The second adjustment estimates depreciation of plant and equipment on a current replacement cost basis rather than on a historic or original cost basis (the way most companies keep their books). The reason for these adjustments is to get a more accurate estimate of cash flow in an economic sense rather than in a conventional accounting sense. Corporate cash flow is regularly reported as a part of the quarterly GNP reports on corporate profits.

A somewhat different and better adjustment can be made to these figures when they are reported. Considerable research has revealed that corporate directors consider the maintenance of a regular dividend rate or payout rate of corporate earnings more important than capital expenditures. Consequently, a significant figure to watch is *net* cash flow, which is the sum of undistributed profits (i.e., profits after dividend distributions) and capital consumption allowances adjusted to a replacement cost basis.

Figure 5.6 compares this corporate net cash flow with nonresidential fixed investment for the years 1950 to 1990. As the figure indicates, internally generated cash flow has not equaled nonresidential fixed investment in any of these years. The differences are accounted for by corporate external financing, by fixed investment of noncorporate entities that is includ-

---

[3]Inventory profits occur in a period of rising prices when inventory purchased earlier at less than prevailing prices is used in production and the company uses a first in/first out (FIFO) method of inventory valuation. The cost of production is understated and artificially inflates profits, because the inventory used up will have to be replaced at a higher cost.

Figure 5.6.   Nonresidential Fixed Investment versus Corporate Cash Flow

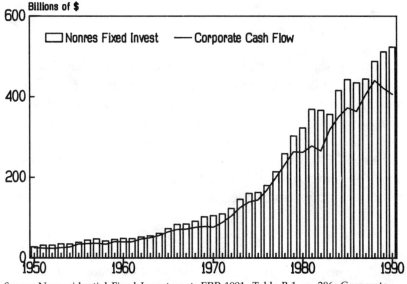

Source: Nonresidential Fixed Investment: ERP 1991, Table B-1, p. 286. Corporate Cash Flow: SCB February 1991, Table 1.14, p. 9; earlier data in earlier issues of SCB and NIPA, Table 1.14 pps. 47–48.

ed in the investment expenditures, or by corporate managers viewing net cash flow in an accounting and not an economic sense.

During this period, corporate cash flow accounted for about 82 percent of nonresidential fixed investment. In 1989, it accounted for approximately 82 percent, and for 1990 the coverage fell to about 78 percent. Continued erosion of this coverage is further evidence supporting expectations of diminished business investment in 1991.

BUSINESS INVENTORIES

The second form of business investment is reflected in the data on business inventories—their changes, their level in relationship to sales, and their relationship to cycles in business activity.

Inventory Cycles

An oversimplified and exaggerated example may illustrate the significance of inventories in causing cycles in business activity. Assume a company has a fairly steady demand of 100 units a month for a product that it manufactures. In order to meet this demand, the company produces 100 units a month and keeps 100 units in inventory in various stages of fabrication. The company's inventory-to-sales ratio therefore is 1, one month's supply, which the company has found by experience to be a satisfactory level.

Now assume that demand picks up to 150 units a month. The 100 units in inventory are now only two-thirds of a month's supply, so that production must be increased to 200 a month (150 units to meet the higher level of demand and another 50 units to restore the inventory-to-sales ratio to 1 again). In short, production has to be doubled on a 50 percent increase in demand. Of course, the reverse is true; if demand fell to 50 units, inventories on hand would represent two month's supply, so that production would have to be cut back sharply to accommodate the lowered level of demand and to reduce a now bloated level of inventories. The correction process is further exaggerated because of the uncertainty before managers can determine whether the latest increase or decrease in demand is temporary or more permanent. Consequently, action to increase or decrease production is delayed and then overcorrected.

This effect of inventories on production, which does not occur in service industries that do not make a product, explains the greater volatility in output of companies that produce goods and why inventory cycles are the most frequent (although not the only) causes of cycles in economic activity.

Measuring GNP Inventory Change

Economists follow two separate statistical series to monitor business inventories. One is contained in the quarterly reports of GNP, which reflects quarter-to-quarter *changes* in business inventories at seasonally adjusted annual rates. The second measure is a monthly series covering total business (i.e., manufacturing, wholesale trade, and retail trade) sales and inventories.

The manner of reporting these two series differs. In the quarterly GNP release, the change in inventories is reported. If more goods are produced than are consumed, the excess is reported as an increase in business inventories and is included in the GNP total as a part of the product during that period. However, if more inventory is consumed than produced, it reflects a reduction in output for the period. Similarly, if the rate of increase in inventories slackens from one quarter to the next, it causes a slowing in the economy's rate of increase. However, the opposite is true if inventory building accelerates.

In the GNP inventory data, the Commerce Department seeks to measure the value of inventory changes expressed in current dollars for a particular reporting period and also in constant 1982 dollars. Consequently, some adjustment is required because businesses have various ways of reporting the value of their inventories. Most companies value inventory on a FIFO basis, i.e., the cost of the oldest inventory on hand is used in accounting for the cost of goods sold. As a result, when prices are rising, inventories held in stock would rise in value even if no change occurred in the physical volume, because the lower cost inventory has been replaced by higher cost inventory.

However, in the GNP accounts, when the data are expressed in current dollar rather than constant 1982 dollars, the intent is to report the physical change in inventories, valued in prices that prevailed during a particular period. The constant dollar series reflects the change in the physical volume of inventories. Therefore, the Commerce Department adjusts the values of business inventories reported to them to the values required in the national income accounts. This adjustment also becomes a measure of inventory profit on the income side of the accounts, which will be considered again when measuring corporate profits.

Figures 5.7 and 5.8 indicate two different ways of looking at business inventory changes in the GNP accounts. Figure 5.7 shows the quarterly change in business inventories from 1953 through 1990. The volatility is evident, indicating why changes in inventories cause most of the fluctuations in business activity. The periods when inventories were actually liquidated (1953, 1957, 1960, 1974, 1980, and 1981) were all years of cyclical contraction. The only period of contraction that was not accom-

Figure 5.7.   Changes in Business Inventories—1982 dollars

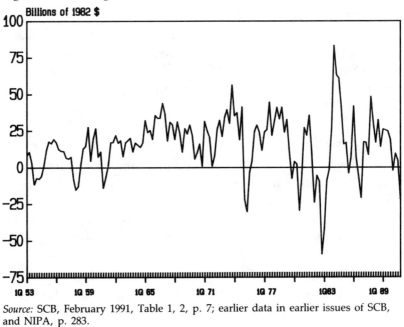

Source: SCB, February 1991, Table 1, 2, p. 7; earlier data in earlier issues of SCB, and NIPA, p. 283.

Figure 5.8.   Real GNP and Final Sales Percent Change

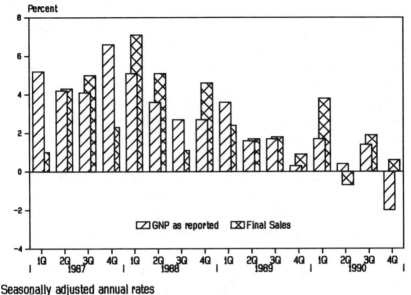

Seasonally adjusted annual rates

Source: SCB February 1991, Table 8.1, p. 20; earlier data in earlier issues of SCB.

panied by an actual liquidation of inventories was 1970, when inventory change was close to zero.

Figure 5.8 indicates the quarter-to-quarter percent changes (at annual rates) in GNP including and excluding the change in business inventories. This figure is similar to Figure 2.1, with one addition. The front bar represents the quarterly percentage change in GNP. The partly concealed bar reflects the quarterly percentage change excluding the change in business inventories, so that it reflects the change in final sales or final demand only. The difference between the two, of course, reflects the change in inventories. Some of the quarterly changes are similar, but others are different. The final sales changes are considered a better indicator of underlying demand in the economy and therefore are watched just as carefully as the changes in total GNP.

Business Sales and Inventories

The second way inventories are reported is in the vast array of information released monthly by the Commerce Department on business sales and inventories. These series cover about 70 percent of all inventories held in the economy; inventories excluded are primarily agricultural and those found in the construction industry. The information is released about 45 days after the end of the month to which it refers. Unlike the GNP inventory figures, these figures are not corrected for any appreciation or depreciation that may have occurred because of changing prices, so that inventory profits and losses are reflected in the totals.

If monthly percent changes in both sales and inventories are plotted, the data fluctuate considerably. Nevertheless, monthly changes are the usual method of communicating this information in the financial press; needless to say, a one-month change in this series should not be given too much weight. In Figure 5.9, the monthly data has been smoothed out by taking a three-month moving average of percentage changes and plotting them. The data are still erratic; nevertheless, it appears that inventory changes are greater in the months after a rise in sales; not unexpected development. However, it is difficult from this type of chart to determine whether inventories are excessive or not.

A more useful way of appraising the level of inventories is to examine the ratio of inventories to sales, which provides an idea of how many months inventories would last at current sales rates if inventories were not replaced. Figure 5.10 presents this information for total business, manufacturing, and retail levels for the period 1987 to 1990. The ratio for total business appears to have trended downward from mid-1989 to August 1990, indicating no significant buildup of inventories during that period. Thereafter, a rapid increase occurred in the

Figure 5.9.   Change in Business Sales and Inventories

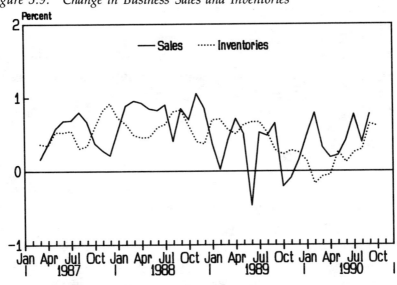

Lines are 3 month moving averages

Source: SCB, February 1991, pps. S-2, S-3; earlier data direct from Bureau of Economic Analysis, U.S. Department of Commerce. Computations by author.

Figure 5.10.   Ratios of Inventories to Sales

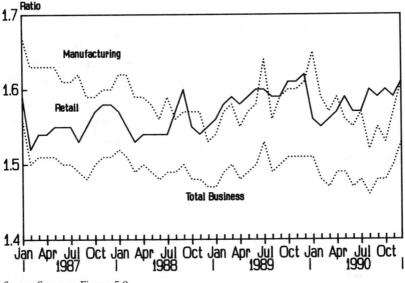

Source: Same as Figure 5.9.

ratio. Retail inventory-to-sales ratios increased from early
1990. By the standards of the 1987 to 1990 period, the levels of
the ratios do not appear excessive, but the rapid increases
toward the end of 1990 suggest that a potential problem may be
building.

MANUFACTURING

Concern is often expressed about the "decline" in U.S.
manufacturing and the unwholesome change from a production to a service economy. However, the manufacturing sector
of the economy contributes about the same percent of the total
output of the economy now as it did three decades ago—about
20 percent of GNP expressed in constant dollars. The shrinking
has occurred on the input side, not the output side. Due to
rising productivity, manufacturing employment has never exceeded the peak of about 21 million workers reached in 1979.
Employment in the service industries has exceeded manufacturing employment since late in the nineteenth century.

Manufacturing is still at the core of our industrial economy, where the efficient production of goods needed permits
the growth of other sectors, including services. Manufacturing
is also important because some 60 percent of exports and 70
percent of imports are classified as goods. Moreover, as indicated earlier, fluctuations in inventories of goods are an important cause of cycles in business activity.

Industrial Production

Statistics on manufacturing are followed carefully as a clue
to the future path of the economy. One of the most carefully
watched series is the monthly industrial production index prepared and released by the Federal Reserve Board. This index

measures the physical output of manufacturing, mining, and utilities, relating them to a base year of 1987. In the index, manufacturing industries account for approximately 84 percent of the weight, with both mining and utilities accounting for 8 percent each. The index is also divided by major markets, such as consumer durable and nondurable goods, business and other equipment, and intermediate products and materials. Several special breakdowns are also prepared. The largest part of the index is based on production of actual items, another part on electric consumption of producing industries, and the balance on production work hours in producing industries.

Figure 5.11 presents the monthly changes in the industrial production index from 1987 through 1990 (dotted line). A three-month moving average (solid line) is plotted because of

Figure 5.11.   % Change in Industrial Production Index

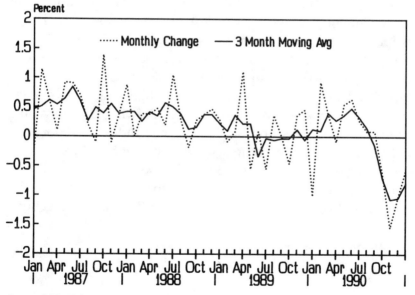

Source: SCB, February 1991, p. S-1; earlier data in earlier issues of SCB and BS, p. 3.

the considerable volatility in the month-to-month changes. If manufacturing were also plotted, it would track the total index very well. The rapid deterioration in the index from mid-1990 was a clear indication that a contraction in business activity was imminent. The change was still negative at the end of 1990, although the rate of fall was slowing.

Purchasing Managers' Index

Another index with a particularly good forecasting record for both manufacturing and the total economy that is available early each month is contained in the *Report on Business* issued by the National Association of Purchasing Management, Tempe, Arizona. The report is widely reported in the financial press.

The participants are about 300 members of the association, and they are selected to parallel closely each manufacturing industry's contribution to GNP. Responses from each member are given equal weight, regardless of company size. Each participant is asked to compare this month's activity with that of the previous month with respect to production, new orders, prices, inventories, supplier deliveries, employment, and exports and imports—up, down, or no change. From these replies, a composite index is prepared showing the prevailing direction and the scope of change. The index may fluctuate between 0 and 100 percent, with an index of 50 percent showing no change. An index reading below 50 percent indicates contraction in the manufacturing sector of the economy. Research on historical relationships between replies and general business conditions reveals that a reading below 43.8 percent is a sign of a general economic contraction.

Figure 5.12 presents the monthly readings in the index from January through December 1990. Contraction in manufacturing was evident from the spring of 1989, with only a temporary uptick in the second quarter of 1990. The subsequent

Figure 5.12.　Purchasing Managers' Index

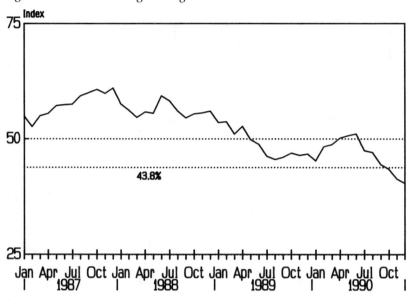

Source: Direct from National Association of Purchasing Management, Tempe, AZ; latest data as reported in *Wall Street Journal*.

deterioration was substantial, and an economic contraction was signaled in October 1990.

Durable Goods New Orders

About one week after the industrial production index is released, the Department of Commerce issues an estimate of the dollar value of new orders for durable goods for the previous month. This series is watched because it has been a leading indicator of business-cycle turning points at both peaks and troughs. New orders are important because they provide a forecast of future manufacturing activity. Unfortunately, this first approximation is just a rough measure and is frequently revised when manufacturing new orders, sales, and inventory

Figure 5.13.   Durable Goods New Orders

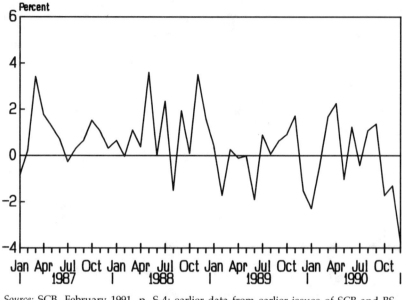

Source: SCB, February 1991, p. S-4; earlier data from earlier issues of SCB and BS, p. 229.

data are released about a week later. Moreover, the series is volatile, making it difficult to determine trends.

Figure 5.13 plots durable goods new orders monthly from 1987 to 1990. To remove some of the volatility, a three-month moving average has been plotted. In 1989 and 1990 the number of decreases was larger than in 1987 and 1988. Moreover, the sharp drop toward the end of 1990 clearly marked a shift in the order pattern. Both of these moves indicated a contraction in activity toward the end of the year.

SUMMARY

The essentials of following business fixed investment, business sales and inventories, and the manufacturing component of the business sector were discussed in this chapter.

Although it accounts for a smaller percent of GNP than does the consumer, the business sector gets a greater degree of analytical attention. Cyclical movements in the business sector are considerably greater than in other areas of the economy. Anticipating these movements can provide clues to future changes in employment, payrolls, retail sales, interest rates, and stock prices.

Some of the data for analyzing the business sector are monthly and current. Other data are available less frequently but are also of significance. The following list provides the monthly and quarterly series discussed in this chapter. The most timely data for short-term business analysis are marked with an ''*''

Business Fixed Investment:

> Nonresidential fixed investment (monthly as a part of the quarterly GNP report);

> Capacity utilization (mid-month for previous month)*;

> Nondefense capital goods, new orders and shipments, inventories, and backlogs (end of month for previous month, updated about ten days later)*;

> Survey of business spending plans (December, April, June, September);

> Business cash flow (available as a part of the second and third monthly estimates of quarterly GNP and its components).

Business Inventories:

> Business sales and inventories and their components (monthly about six weeks after the end of the reported month)*;

Change in business inventories (monthly as a part of the report on quarterly GNP).

Manufacturing:

Purchasing managers' report (monthly at beginning of month)*;

Industrial production (monthly at mid month)*;

Durable goods new orders (monthly toward the end of the month, updated about ten days later)*.

CHAPTER 6

The World Overseas

American economic relations with the rest of the world have received a lot of attention in recent years. The United States has increasingly become a part of the world economy. The trade deficit, foreign ownership of U.S. companies and real estate, and calls for protectionist legislation in Congress make the headlines. News is transmitted instantly. Money can move just as quickly, and investments are made daily—on a national as well as on a global basis.

This chapter will cover only the part of U.S. international relationships that deals with the performance of the U.S. economy in foreign trade, foreign investment, and the dollar in international exchange markets. The major concepts discussed are:

Balance of payments. The measure of the flow of goods, services income, and unilateral transfers between the United States and countries overseas, as well as the flow of funds back and forth to pay for them;

Balance on current account. That portion of the balance of payments that measures the flows of goods, services income, and unilateral transfers;

Net exports of goods and services. That part of the quarterly GNP reports that measures the exports and imports of goods, services income, and investment income;

Merchandise trade. The flow of exports and imports of goods alone and the only part of the balance of payments reported monthly;

Offsetting capital flows. Reported as *increases* or *decreases* in U.S. assets abroad and in foreign assets in the United States. The *value* of these assets in the United States and abroad is also reported;

Direct investments in the United States and abroad. Investment in industrial plants, commercial and residential property, and other physical assets.

Dollar in international trade. This trade is denominated primarily in dollars. The exchange value of the dollar can be measured directly against other currencies and also by an index weighted by the average world trade of ten major trading countries. The effects of the dollar's exchange movements on trade and investment as well as on monetary policy of the U.S. and foreign central banks are discussed because of their importance in foreign trade.

BALANCE OF PAYMENTS

Merchandise exports and imports account for approximately three-quarters of the dollars in U.S. international transactions. However, other transactions also cause funds to flow between the United States and countries overseas. Some funds flow abroad unilaterally, such as pensions paid to Americans living overseas, or remittances and gifts sent abroad by U.S. residents or to U.S. residents from abroad. Investment income, fees, royalties, and military transactions flow both ways. Finally, U.S. capital investments are made abroad and foreign investments are made in the United States; these assets ultimately result in income flows back and forth.

When overseas obligations of the United States are matched against foreign obligations to the United States, a surplus or deficit exists. This surplus or deficit is balanced out in the case of a surplus by the United States investing or loaning funds overseas; if a deficit exists, it is offset by foreign loans or investments in the United States. The measure of these flows of goods and services between the United States and overseas is reflected in the *balance of payments accounts.*

The balance of payments accounts provide two kinds of information. The first reflects foreign trade in goods, services income, and unilateral transfers. The second reflects the money and capital flows used to finance trade, transfers, and grants. Theoretically the two should match, but because of inadequate statistical data a "statistical discrepancy" is used to make up the difference. The balance of payments data are issued quarterly by the Department of Commerce about 75 days after the end of the quarter to which they refer. They are published in the April, June, September, and December issues of the Department of Commerce monthly publication, *Survey of Current Business.*

Components

The components of the balance of payments is summarized in the following list.

Exports of goods, services and income, consisting of three parts:

Merchandise trade;

Services, including travel costs, royalties, and other private services;

Income received from U.S. assets owned abroad.

Imports of goods, services, and income, which has three parts:

Merchandise trade;

Services, including direct defense expenditures overseas, travel costs, royalties, and other private services;

Income payments from foreign assets owned in the United States.

Unilateral transfers, net, including transfers, or flows of funds, into and out of the United States:

U.S. government grants, pensions, and other government transfers;

Private remittances and other private transfers.

The capital flows that offset these three components are as follows:

Net increase or decrease in U.S. assets abroad, reflected by changes in:

U.S. official reserve assets, including gold, special drawing rights, and the reserve position in the International Monetary Fund (IMF) plus foreign currency holdings;

Other U.S. government assets held abroad, including loans to foreign nations, capital contributions to international organizations except the IMF, and other holdings of foreign currencies;

U.S. private assets held abroad, including direct investment, foreign security holdings, and claims on foreigners.

Net increase or decrease in foreign assets in the United States reflected by changes in:

Foreign official (government or government entities) assets owned in the United States, including foreign holdings of U.S. government securities, corporate debt and equity securities, and of state and local governments;

Other foreign assets, including U.S. government as well as private securities, and direct investment in U.S. assets;

Other liabilities to foreigners.

The quarterly report on the balance of payments has a wealth of information on U.S. international transactions, much of which is of a specialized nature. For the purposes of tracking the U.S. business picture, however, focus should be concentrated on the three major summary reports that are usually communicated in one way or another in the financial press:

Balance on current account. A quarterly report that includes exports and imports of goods, services and income, plus net unilateral transfers;

Net exports of goods and services. Reported as a part of the quarterly GNP accounts;

Balance on merchandise trade. The only component of the balance of payments report available monthly.

BALANCE ON CURRENT ACCOUNT

The report on the balance on current account reflects the net difference between exports and imports of goods, services and income, combined with the net difference between unilateral transfers that occur between the United States and the rest of the world.

Figure 6.1 plots this information for the 1981 to 1989 period. The segment of each bar above the zero line reflects that part of the current account where the United States received

Figure 6.1.   U.S. Balance on Current Account

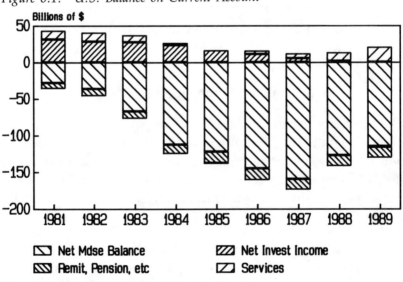

Source: ERB 1991, Table B-102, p. 402.

more than it sent overseas. The amount below the zero line represents a deficit for the United States. The legend at the bottom of the Figure identifies the components involved. For example, in 1981 U.S. net investment income from abroad, totaled approximately $31 billion, which more than offset the U.S. merchandise trade deficit of about $28 billion. However, this investment income from abroad decreased until, by 1989, it was a small net outflow instead of an inflow. On the other side, the merchandise trade deficit increased until 1987 and was primarily responsible for making the current account deficit that year the largest in U.S. history. Shrinking of the trade deficit and increased services income improved the current account deficit in 1988 to 1989, although it still remained negative.

NET EXPORTS OF GOODS AND SERVICES

Net exports of goods and services are reported as one of the parts of the quarterly GNP reports; they are given in both current and constant dollars. The information includes not only merchandise trade, but also services income and investment income; unilateral transfers are excluded. This series is monitored because it is an inclusive measure of current external economic transactions that affect the U.S. economy.

Figure 6.2 places exports and imports in current dollars into perspective by relating them to GNP for the 1950 to 1990 period. The net export line at the bottom of the figure generally fluctuated between zero and plus 2 percent of GNP until 1983. Until then, net exports fluctuated so little and were so modest in size relative to the whole economy that they received little attention in business forecasts.

Two developments changed that focus. Beginning in the early 1970s, exports and imports, taken separately, increased as

Figure 6.2.   Exports and Imports as a Percent GNP

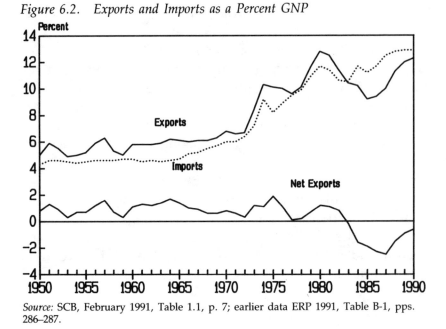

Source: SCB, February 1991, Table 1.1, p. 7; earlier data ERP 1991, Table B-1, pps. 286–287.

Figure 6.3.   Net Exports of Goods and Services

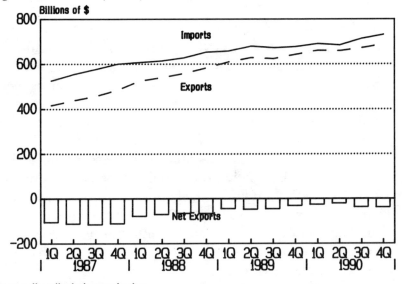

Seasonally adjusted annual rates

Source: SCB, February 1991, Table 1.1, p. 7; earlier data ERP 1991, Table B-1, p. 287, BS, pps. 276–277.

Figure 6.4. Monthly Merchandise Trade Deficit

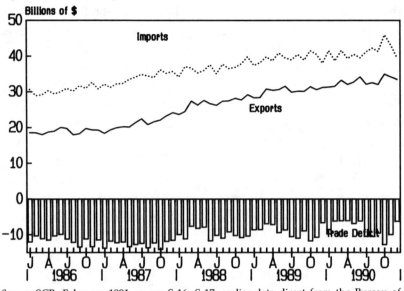

Source: SCB, February 1991, pages S-16, S-17; earlier data direct from the Bureau of the Census, U.S. Department of Commerce.

a percent of GNP. In addition, net exports were in deficit in 1983 for the first time since 1945. This deficit fell to 2.5 percent of GNP in 1987; the percent has improved since but still is negative.

Figure 6.3 provides a quarterly picture of exports, imports, and net exports quarterly from 1987 through 1990. The narrowing of the trade deficit from the third quarter of 1987 through the second quarter of 1989 is evident. The events in the Middle East impacted oil import costs during the third and fourth quarters of 1990 and were primarily responsible for the increase in the deficit in those quarters.

MERCHANDISE TRADE BALANCE

Figure 6.4 provides a picture of merchandise trade, the major portion of the net exports of goods and services (merchandise trade accounts for about 60 percent of exports and 68 percent of imports; service and investment income account for the remainder). The data are monthly from 1986 through 1990. This monthly figure, released by the Department of Commerce about 45 days after the end of the month to which it refers, is probably the most carefully watched of the total balance of payments statistics.[1] The month-to-month changes in the trade data are erratic and large. Consequently, plotting the monthly dollar amounts for both exports and imports for several years and revising prior months' data when available is a better way to analyze the movements.

When examined this way, as shown by the bars at the bottom of Figure 6.4, the gradual improvement from the fall of 1987 through mid-1990 is evident, as is the deterioration since mid-1990. Future outlook for the trade deficit can be estimated more accurately after an examination of the changes in the composition of exports and imports over a longer period of time.

Figure 6.5 indicates the major components of U.S. *exports* in 1970 versus 1989. (More recent data were not available at the time of this writing.) As the note in the figure indicates, U.S. exports increased 8.3 times during this period; by comparison, GNP grew 5.1 times. The major changes in composition were twofold: on one hand, a drop in the percentage of exports in food, related products, and industrial supplies; on the other hand, an increase in capital goods excluding automobiles and consumer goods. The increase in capital goods was due in part to an increase in aircraft sales.

Figure 6.6 indicates the changing nature of *imports* during the 1970 to 1989 period; imports increased 11.8 times versus the

[1]Business inventory statistics for all of the months of the quarter are not available until shortly before the second estimate of the quarterly GNP data, and full net export information is not available until shortly before the third estimate. The changes in these two volatile areas account for most of the revisions between the first and last estimate of GNP for a particular quarter.

Figure 6.5.   U.S. Merchandise Exports 1970 versus 1989

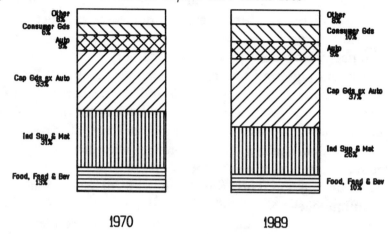

1989 U.S. Exports were 8.3 times 1970
Source: ERP, 1991, Table B-103, p. 404.

Figure 6.6.   U.S. Merchandise Imports 1970 versus 1989

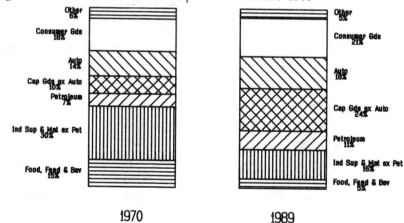

1989 U.S. Imports were 11.8 times 1970
Source: Same as Figure 6.5

5.1 times increase in GNP during that period. The increases reflected increased purchases of automotive products, business, office machines and electronic products, as well as the manufacture of more parts and machinery abroad. American consumers preferred foreign goods either because of price or quality; many U.S. companies found it cheaper to produce parts or products abroad. The increased value of petroleum products imports was due to a combination of higher consumption and higher prices. The percentage-point increase in petroleum imports was not as great as that of capital goods excluding automobiles and just equal to the percentage-point increase in automobiles. Nevertheless, the dollar value of petroleum imports is quite volatile, and the 1990 to 1991 conflict in the Persian Gulf intensified that volatility. The decreases came in agricultural products and industrial supplies.

As the nature of U.S. imports shifted, so did the countries from which the imports came. In 1970, 28 percent of U.S. imports came from Canada, 15 percent from Japan, 8 percent from the United Kingdom, and 6 percent from Germany. In 1989, 20 percent came from Japan and another 26 percent from other Asian and African countries that were not even reported separately in 1970. Cars and electronic gear as well as apparel and textile products were the major imports from Asian countries. By 1989, Canadian imports had decreased to 19 percent of the total, while the United Kingdom decreased to 4 percent and Germany remained steady at about 5 percent.

Predicting the future of the U.S. trade deficit is not easy. The imports from Asian countries will be difficult to dislodge, given the desire of U.S. consumers for Asian products that are considered either of better quality or cheaper than U.S. products. This is offset by the decline in the value of the dollar in foreign exchange (discussed later in this chapter) which makes foreign goods more expensive and U.S. goods more competitive abroad. In addition, U.S. corporations are becoming more competitive in international trade, in both price and quality of goods.

Enacting protectionist legislation is not likely to help; it could lead to retaliatory legislation abroad and lower foreign trade generally. The present process of patient negotiations with each country, working to change trade practices and reduce barriers, is more likely to contribute to an improvement in the U.S. trade deficit.

OFFSETTING CAPITAL FLOWS

Increases or decreases in U.S. assets abroad and of foreign assets in the United States are the means of financing the foreign trade in goods and services as well as unilateral transfers. Figure 6.7 shows the annual increases (denominated in

Figure 6.7. Asset Flows from and to the United States

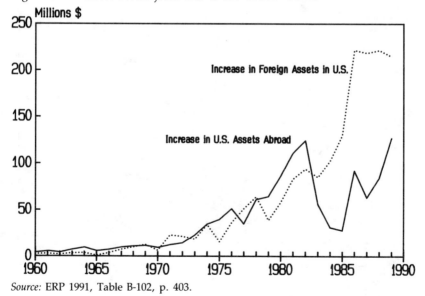

Source: ERP 1991, Table B-102, p. 403.

dollars) in U.S. assets abroad and in foreign assets in the United States from 1960 through 1989. The year-to-year increase in U.S. assets abroad kept pace with the year-to-year increase of foreign assets in the United States until 1982. The deterioration in the U.S. current account after 1982, as shown in Figure 6.1, resulted in a significant rate of increase in foreign assets in the United States, while the growth of U.S. assets abroad slowed. Since 1985, the rate of decline in the U.S. net investment position of the United States has slowed; however, the outflow is still negative.

A more dramatic illustration of this change is shown in Figure 6.8, indicating the value expressed in dollars of U.S. assets abroad compared with the value of foreign assets held in the United States. The value of foreign assets in the United States has exceeded U.S. asset holdings abroad since 1984. These figures, however, should be interpreted with caution.

Figure 6.8. U.S. International Investment Position

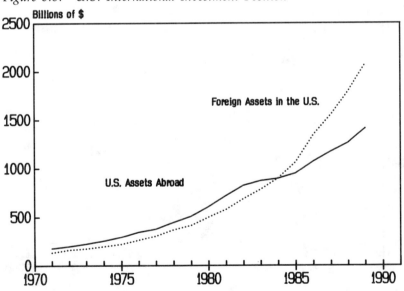

Source: SCB, June 1990, Table 1, p. 55.

The Commerce Department points out that many of these assets are valued on a historical cost basis. Consequently, the more recently acquired foreign assets in the United States have a higher cost basis than the older U.S. assets held abroad. If all assets were valued at current prices, U.S. asset holdings would probably still exceed foreign assets in value. Nevertheless, the trends in favor of overseas holdings of U.S. assets are likely to continue.

One other measure is worth considering. Figure 6.9 compares the dollar value of U.S. direct investments abroad with foreign direct investments in the United States. *Direct investments* reflect investment in industrial plants, commercial and residential property, as well as other physical assets. It is worth mentioning that in 1989 direct investments represented about 26 percent of U.S. assets held overseas but 19 percent of foreign assets held in the United States. The bulk of investments are in financial assets such as bank loans, bonds, and stocks.

Figure 6.9.   Foreign versus U.S. Direct Investments

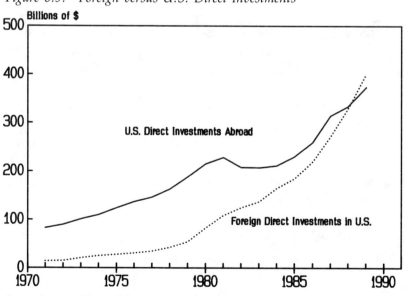

Source: Same as Figure 6.8.

The total amount of foreign direct investment in the United States was about $401 billion in 1989. Of this, 65 percent was accounted for by European countries. The United Kingdom accounted for 30 percent, the Netherlands 15 percent, and other European countries the remaining 20 percent. The second largest country in direct investment after the United Kingdom was Japan, with 17 percent of total direct investment. These data are reported annually in great detail by the Department of Commerce and published in the *Survey of Current Business*.

DIRECT INVESTMENTS

What has caused foreign investment and ownership of assets in the United States to grow? The primary cause is the significant increase in the United States trade deficit during the past several years, which put a large amount of dollars in foreign hands. Foreigners, having more and more dollars, have invested a large portion of these dollars in the United States. Such action is especially likely if foreigners see a stable economy, low inflation, and better returns than are available in their own countries. These trends will continue until the U.S. trade deficit is reduced significantly or U.S. investment becomes relatively less attractive.

Is foreign investment in the United States sufficiently large to give overseas investors significant market power in the U.S. economy? Recent studies have concluded that no great threat is seen from the size of current holdings. Any measure of superiority foreign-owned companies have comes more from their competitive advantages than their ownership. Moreover, the United States has antitrust laws and other regulations that prevent unfair competition, which are equally applicable to firms owned by overseas investors.

Foreign ownership has contributed to U.S. employment, technology, capital flows, and a more competitive environment, all of which have been good for this country. It should be remembered that the United States was a debtor nation until the turn of the century, and investment from overseas prior to that time contributed a great deal to the early economic development of the United States. Subsequent U.S. investment abroad has helped develop economies overseas, and has reaped benefits through investment income from this free flow of capital worldwide.

Restrictions on capital flows, such as trade restrictions, are not reasonable solutions to the challenge of foreign ownership or investment. Such moves invite retaliation and further restrictions on trade and capital flows, and ultimately can only harm the economies of the countries that participate. (One exception where foreign ownership should be restricted, however, is the defense area, where national interests should mandate domestic control of U.S. companies.)

Foreign ownership is not an isolated problem but rather part of many problems involved in an intertwined, complex international world. As part of that interdependence, the views of foreign investors, central banks and governments regarding U.S. political and economic policies are now very important. The flow of investment funds from abroad indicates that thus far the evaluation is more positive than negative. Should this flow of funds slow or stop, the funds now provided from overseas will have to be raised in the United States. Higher interest rates would result from increased competition for funds. In the long term, a lower U.S. standard of living could result as we pay interest and dividends on, as well as repay the principal of, our overseas debt. Foreign ownership is a symptom of the disease of the U.S. trade and federal deficits—these, rather than foreign ownership, are the real causes of concern.

THE DOLLAR

An issue closely related to international trade is the value of the U.S. dollar in foreign exchange. Why, since 1971, when exchange rates were free to fluctuate, have the dollar's movements become increasingly important to the U.S. consumer and of major importance to the U.S. investor?

International trade is denominated primarily in U.S. dollars (crude oil is a good example). Direct foreign investment in the United States requires dollars. Overseas portfolio investments are made in dollar-denominated securities by central banks and other institutional investors. Large dollar-denominated capital markets exist overseas. Therefore, fluctuations in the dollar have international repercussions.

The dollar, as do most major currencies, trades relatively freely in foreign exchange markets, its value rising and falling with the demand and supply provided by buyers and sellers. Increasing dollar fluctuations distort the terms of international trade, so that central banks at times intervene in these markets, but their purchases and sales are designed only to stabilize currency markets.

In the past 20 years, a significant amount of dollars has flowed abroad, changing the United States from a creditor to the world's largest debtor nation. One reason for the flow was the very substantial increase in the price of crude oil, beginning in 1973. This increase transferred a significant portion of wealth into the hands of the oil-producing countries. Overseas lending by U.S. banks caused an additional accumulation of dollars in foreign hands. Also, as pointed out earlier, the American consumer developed a strong taste for foreign goods, resulting in a growing trade deficit. Finally, and by no means the least important, large federal budget deficits led to fears of inflation, and the Federal Reserve instituted a tight monetary policy that ultimately broke the back of inflation while sending interest rates to record highs. These higher rates attracted funds to the United States from overseas.

Foreigners were willing to hold and add to their dollar holdings, thus bidding up the dollar's value relative to other currencies. Comparable U.S. assets were selling at prices lower than prices elsewhere. Foreign investment, both in real assets and securities, was attracted to the United States because interest rates were higher than those available at home. The demand for dollars drove its value up relative to other currencies until 1985. At that point, foreign concern about the U.S. budget deficit, trade deficit, and political fights over the budget deficit started a decline in the dollar's value; by the end of 1987 the dollar was down almost 50 percent against major currencies.

The exchange rate of the dollar against most major currencies can be found in the financial section of most newspapers. The rates are usually reported in two ways:

The U.S. dollar equivalent of each unit of a foreign currency; and

The amount of a foreign currency that is equal to one U.S. dollar.

These exchange rates usually apply to rates for trading among banks in amounts of $1 million or more. Smaller transactions provide fewer units of foreign currency per dollar. In discussions of particular currencies, the British pound and the Canadian dollar are usually quoted in terms of how much is needed in U.S. dollars to buy a unit of that currency, for example, $1.9530 is required to buy one pound. Other currencies are usually quoted in terms of the amount of their currency required to purchase a U.S. dollar, for example, 132.70 yen or 1.4920 German marks are needed to buy one dollar.

Other methods are used to measure the value of the dollar relative to other currencies. Figure 6.10 plots the exchange

Figure 6.10.   Exchange Value of the U.S. Dollar

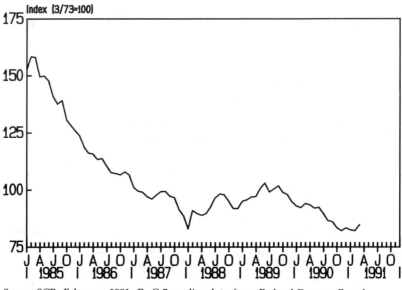

Source: SCB, February 1991, P. C-5; earlier data from Federal Reserve Board Division of Research and Statistics.

value of the dollar against a group of other major currencies monthly from 1985 through early 1991 in terms of an index number. The index is a weighted average exchange value of the U.S. dollar against the currencies of ten industrial countries. The weight for each of the countries is the 1972 to 1976 average world trade of that country divided by the average world trade of all ten countries combined.

Using this measure, the dollar fell from a peak in February 1985 to a low in January 1988. The recovery until mid-1989 was due to some improvement in the U.S. trade deficit, but more important, U.S. interest rates were higher than those abroad, and the United States was a safe haven and a more attractive place for investment than alternative nations. The dollar resumed its downtrend beginning in mid-1989 and by the end of 1990 had reached the 1988 low; a slight recovery occurred in early 1991. Failure to come to grips with the federal budget deficit, a sluggish U.S. economy, more attractive investment opportunities abroad, and falling U.S. interest rates have all contributed to a lower dollar value, making the United States less attractive for overseas investment.

Effects of Dollar Movements

Movements in the foreign exchange value of the dollar have an effect on U.S. international trade, the U.S. economy, interest rates, and investments generally. Fluctuations in the value of the dollar in foreign exchange are caused by a complex mixture of actions by diverse participants with different objectives who may have different perceptions of the global political and economic environment.

What are the effects of the dollar *rising* relative to other currencies? (The effects are the opposite if the dollar is weak, as it was in 1990.) Essentially, a stronger dollar means that someone holding dollars gets more foreign currency per dollar when an exchange is made from dollars to that foreign currency. Clearly, U.S. travelers abroad benefit from a stronger dollar, but some of the broader economic implications are less obvious. Some of these implications are:

Importers who sell goods or services to the United States are paid in dollars and get more of their own currency in exchange. Therefore, they can afford to charge less in dollars for their goods or services, and can be more competitive relative to U.S. providers of similar goods and services. Consequently, imports rise in the U.S. balance of payments accounts. Demand for comparable domestic goods and services is discouraged, and price competition from imports reduces the ability of U.S. companies to increase prices, putting downward pressures on inflation.

Slackening in the economy and downward price pressures may depress interest rates;

U.S. exporters selling their goods and services overseas are paid in foreign currencies and therefore get less dollars when their foreign currencies are exchanged into dollars. U.S. exports must therefore be priced higher or profit margins and profits will be lowered. Exports from the United States are discouraged, exports in the U.S. balance of payments are lower, and the domestic economy is slowed. Downward pressure on U.S. interest rates results because of this slackening in demand;

Foreign investors who hold U.S. investments get more of their domestic currency in income when they convert interest, dividends, and rent from dollars into their own domestic currency when the dollar is appreciating. The value of their U.S. investments also appreciates when translated into their domestic currency. Foreign investment in the United States is attractive, especially if the U.S. dollar is expected to continue to appreciate. Foreigners are willing to invest in the United States as long as they are not concerned about the safety of their investments and do not fear default. Because of the flow of funds to the United States from abroad, pressure on U.S. interest rates is downward;

Foreign investors who want to buy U.S. investments in a strong dollar market must pay more of their own currency to get dollars for the purchase. Therefore, investment in the United States is discouraged *unless* these investors believe that the dollar will continue to appreciate. If foreign investment is discouraged, funds for domestic uses must come from domestic sources, thus exercising upward pressures on interest rates;

U.S. investors who hold foreign investments receive less in dollars of income on their investments; in addition, the value of their overseas investments depreciates when translated into dollars. Investments outside the United States cost more when the dollar is strong and is therefore discouraged. The U.S. trade deficit increases as U.S. goods are less competitive, resulting in reduced income from abroad. However, investments in the United States are more attractive to U.S. corporations, and the greater funds available here puts downward pressures on interest rates;

Oil prices are denominated in dollars; therefore, dollar fluctuations have no effect on the cost of U.S. oil imports. However, other countries need more of their currencies if they buy the necessary dollars to purchase oil, diverting more resources to the purchase of oil and depressing their economies. (This effect has been somewhat modified by the development of barter deals between oil-producing and oil-consuming nations.) A stronger dollar helps oil-producing countries that can buy more foreign goods with the more valuable dollars they receive.

U.S. Monetary Policy

Monetary policy and the operations of the Federal Reserve will be discussed at greater length in Chapter 8. However, because movements of currencies in foreign exchange affect monetary policy, a few brief comments will be made here.

To understand the effects of a stronger dollar on monetary policy in the United States, the principal objectives of the Federal Reserve must be kept in mind:

Restrain inflation in the United States, suggesting that the Federal Reserve would favor a stronger dollar, increasing the competition from imports and exercising downward pressure on inflation and interest rates;

Encourage domestic economic growth, suggesting that the Federal Reserve would favor a weaker dollar, encouraging exports, discouraging imports, and stimulating domestic economic growth;

Maintain foreign investment interest in the United States in order to help finance both trade deficits and budget deficits. (Foreign investors now hold about 15 percent of outstanding federal debt and are significant buyers of new Treasury issues.) If foreign investment is not encouraged, more financing must be done internally, forcing U.S. interest rates up and discouraging U.S. economic growth. Therefore, a stronger dollar encourages foreign investment.

The Federal Reserve is faced with a difficult balancing act. To discourage inflation, the Federal Reserve would favor higher interest rates—but not so high as to discourage economic expansion. To encourage domestic economic growth, the Federal Reserve would like lower interest rates—but not so low as to encourage inflation. To attract foreign investment, the Federal Reserve would like higher interest rates—but not so high as to curtail domestic economic expansion. The choices are difficult, and policy emphasis shifts depending on what particular objective is most important at the time.

Foreign Central Bank Policies

Volatile currency movements are disruptive to international trade and financial transactions; central banks intervene from time to time in foreign exchange markets to dampen these currency fluctuations. However, the funds central banks can devote to currency stability are relatively small compared with the enormous volume of other transactions, so that underlying economic forces will ultimately set the direction of currency movements.

Foreign central banks cooperate with the Federal Reserve in interventions in foreign exchange markets, but their objectives in such cooperation are not necessarily the same. In addition to stabilizing currency fluctuations, foreign central banks have the following considerations in mind:

Contain inflation and encourage economic growth in their own countries, especially by expanding exports, which are more important to the economies of many countries than they are for the United States. Helping the U.S. reduce its trade deficit is of secondary importance;

Because foreign funds loaned to the United States to finance the U.S. trade deficit represent a capital outflow, foreign central banks are willing to help reduce the U.S. trade deficit only to the extent that is not inconsistent with their own domestic objectives;

With respect to exchange rates, a strong dollar is generally preferable because it encourages exports to the United States and because the dollar is still the major reserve currency held by foreign central banks;

U.S. interest rates higher than those in foreign countries encourage outflow of capital, which, unless a country has a very large balance of payments surplus, is not especially desirable;

When foreign central banks are required to support the U.S. dollar by buying it in exchange markets, their purchases are paid for with their domestic currency, which increases supply and is therefore inflationary. Consequently, their willingness to continue dollar support is necessarily limited;

The dollar is not the only currency that concerns foreign central banks; the currency relationships among all of their major trading partners are of concern. Therefore, actions may be taken that are directed at objectives other than just assisting the dollar. Nevertheless, the dollar is still the major currency in international transactions and therefore one that gets the majority of attention.

SUMMARY

This chapter discussed measures of the transactions of the United States with the rest of the world and fluctuations of the dollar in foreign exchange and the effects of these fluctuations on trade, investment, and monetary policy.

The detailed reports of the balance of payments are prepared and published by the Department of Commerce in its monthly publication *Survey of Current Business;* little of this detail is mentioned in the news media. The one part usually reported is the monthly data on merchandise trade; following the movements of exports, imports, and the net trade deficit will track about three-quarters of the dollars in U.S. interna-

Table 6.1.
High and Lows
U.S. Dollar vs. Major Foreign Currencies 1985–1990

	Dollars per Pound	Yen per Dollar	Marks per Dollar
1985 high	1.0546	278.08	3.4375
1987 low	1.8870	121.10	1.5705
1989 high	1.5120	149.46	2.0340
1990 low	1.9830	124.33	1.4700

tional transactions. The data should be reviewed over a number of months because the figures are often revised significantly; the data initially reported for any month should be reviewed for revisions when subsequent month's data are reported.

The movement of the trade-weighted index is not normally covered in the news media, although it is available in the monthly *Federal Reserve Bulletin* and the *Survey of Current Business*. A simple way to track currency movements is to follow the dollar on a daily or weekly basis relative to its value compared with three major currencies: the British pound, the Japanese yen, and the German mark. Movements can be measured against recent highs and lows. Table 6.1 summarizes these dollar highs and lows.

CHAPTER 7

Government and the Economy

Spending for goods and services by federal, state, and local governments now consumes about 20 percent of the nation's output. Therefore, trends and shifts in this spending are factors to be reckoned with in any analysis of business conditions. The role of the government is even greater because of the sums it transfers from one group of people to another as a part of its regular activities. Social security benefits, unemployment insurance, veterans' benefits, and government pension payments are all part of what is called entitlements. *Entitlement payments* are made automatically to individuals who qualify and reflect the transfer of income or assets from one group to another in our society. Another government activity of economic significance is the effect of government borrowing in the financial markets as federal deficits and debt keep growing.

Statistical data to measure government activity are not easily available, although political and social commentary can be found in abundance. This chapter will discuss the data regularly published on government activities. However, the bulk of the chapter will provide background material on spending, the deficit, the federal debt, and the critical issues of the future of social security and medicare. This information may provide the reader with some perspective to interpret current reports and commentary in the media.

The important terms in this chapter are:

Government purchases of goods and services. That part the federal, state, and local governments take of the current output of the economy, or the GNP;

Federal, state, and local expenditures. The *total* amount of government outlays in a particular period. These differ from purchases of goods and services primarily because of *transfer payments.* These payments are not a part of current output but rather represent the transfer of income or wealth (e.g., social security payments and government pensions) from one group to another. Other items not included in purchases are interest on debt, grants, and subsidies;

Federal, state, and local receipts. The income received from various revenue sources, such as income and other types of taxes, social security payments, and unemployment insurance;

Federal deficits. The difference between federal government receipts and expenditures, which is financed by *federal debt,* borrowing both in the United States and abroad.

Methods of issuing this debt have important conse-
quences for economic activity;

The *federal budget*. The government's projection of annual
receipts and expenditures, the difference being either a
surplus (rare) or a *deficit*. The financing of the deficit adds
to the debt. Reducing the deficit is difficult, but a recently
adopted new process offers some hope for improvement.
The *national income and product accounts* (NIPA) provide
more useful ways of tracking government spending than
do budget numbers;

Social security. The system of providing retirement and
disability benefits. Income exceeds payments at this
time—the system is building a surplus placed in a government *trust fund* that, although not included in current
calculations of the budget deficit, is a tempting target for
other federal spending programs. The payment for non-
hospital benefits under *Part B of Medicare* is significantly
less than premiums received and is a growing drain on the
federal treasury.

GOVERNMENT PURCHASES OF GOODS AND SERVICES

Information on *government purchases of goods and services*, by
the federal, state, and local governments, is reported quarterly
as a component of the GNP reports. This information reflects
the amount of the current output of the economy that is absorbed by the government. The federal government accounts
for about 40 percent of total government purchases of goods
and services, with state and local spending accounting for the
balance. Defense spending accounts for about 75 percent of the
federal government purchases.

In order to provide some perspective of the dimensions of
government spending in the economy, Figure 7.1 plots federal,

Figure 7.1.   Government Purchasers of Goods and Services as a Percent of GNP

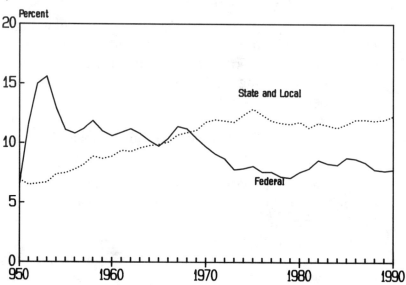

Source: SCB, February 1991, Table 1.1, p. 7; earlier data, ERP 1991, Table B-1, p. 287. Computations by the author.

state, and local spending as a percent of GNP annually from 1950 through 1990. The hump in federal spending for 1951 to 1954 reflects the costs of the Korean War. Viewing spending this way, it appears that federal spending until 1980 was a declining portion of GNP while the state portion increased. In recent years, the trends have been relatively stable. More than half of spending at all levels is for employee compensation, mostly employees of the armed forces at the federal level and education employees at the state and local level.

These figures, while informative, do not measure the totality of government receipts and expenditures, just that portion that is taken from current output. A broader measure that includes *all* government spending is illustrated relative to GNP in Figure 7.2. By this measure, federal spending relative to GNP is the larger of the two and has been rising, peaking out at

Figure 7.2.   Government Expenditures as a Percent of GNP

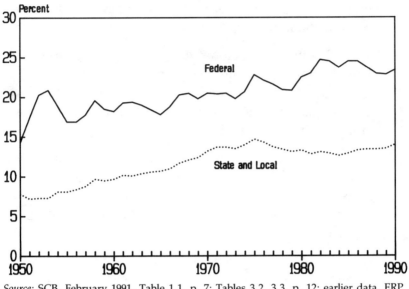

Source: SCB, February 1991, Table 1.1, p. 7; Tables 3.2, 3.3, p. 12; earlier data, ERP 1991, Table B-79, p. 379.

24.7 percent in 1982. State and local spending is smaller; it peaked at 14.7 percent in 1975 but was 14 percent in 1990.

FEDERAL RECEIPTS AND EXPENDITURES

Details on federal receipts and expenditures are available from the Bureau of Economic Analysis of the Department of Commerce and are published in its monthly bulletin, the *Survey of Current Business.* The numbers do not agree precisely with the budget figures reported in the press; instead, they are on a *national income and product account (NIPA)* basis. The differences are as follows:

The federal budget figures are on a fiscal year basis (now October 1 through September 30), while the NIPA figures are on a calendar year basis. Using the NIPA figures enables easier comparisons with other economic data that are on a calendar year basis;

The NIPA figures include *all* government receipts and expenditures. Thus they avoid the confusion created by "on-budget" and "off-budget" categories, which have been used to segregate social security funds when computing the federal deficit;

The NIPA figures are presented at seasonally adjusted annual rates; this is not done for the budget figures. Thus, the NIPA figures can be compared with other statistical measures of the economy that are reported seasonally adjusted;

Some minor differences occur in the budget and the NIPA concepts due to timing and coverage, but for all practical purposes the NIPA figures are satisfactory and are used by most economists to monitor the government sector.

Figure 7.3 plots federal receipts and expenditures from 1950 through 1990. Receipts and expenditures tracked each other closely until the 1970s, with small surpluses in 9 years and small deficits in 11 years. The Vietnam War, President Johnson's Great Society, and President Reagan's defense build-up and tax cuts widened the spread and the 1980s were years of large deficits.

A more detailed examination of receipts and expenditures for several of these years indicate the changing nature of federal receipts and expenditures. Table 7.1 presents details for the years 1950, 1970, and 1990.

Reviewing the receipts side, the two major revenue sources are personal taxes and contributions for social insurance (social security, unemployment insurance, and retirement and pension fund contributions). The largest single source of revenue has been personal income taxes—43 percent. Social

Figure 7.3. Federal Receipts and Expenditures

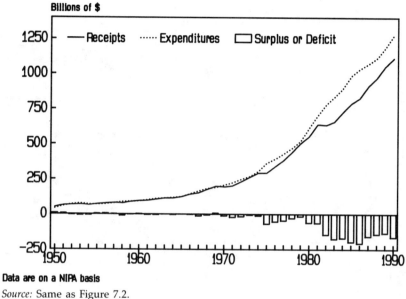

Data are on a NIPA basis

Source: Same as Figure 7.2.

insurance has jumped from 12 percent in 1950 to 40 percent in 1990. Corporate tax accruals have shrunk to 10 percent, and, within that, profits of the Federal Reserve Banks are one-fifth of the total.[1]

The relative weights of the sources of earnings give some idea of where significant revenues can be raised when tax increases are under consideration by Congress. Income and social security taxes are clearly the largest revenue raisers.

On the expenditure side, the purchase of goods and services falls into perspective, accounting in 1990 for approximately one-third of total expenditures. The largest expenditure item was *transfer payments.* Those payments include

[1]The Federal Reserve Banks are included because their stock is owned by the nation's banks that are members of the system. However, after paying a 6 percent dividend to the stockholders, about 95 percent of the net earnings are paid into the U.S. Treasury.

Table 7.1.
Federal Government Receipts and Expenditures—1950, 1970, and 1990

	1950	1970	1990	1950 Percent	1970 Percent	1990 Percent
	(Billions of Dollars)					
Receipts						
Personal Tax and Other Receipts	18.1	92.6	492.8	35.9	47.4	44.3
Income Taxes	17.4	88.8	479.1	34.5	45.4	43.1
Estate and Gift Taxes	0.6	3.7	11.7	1.2	1.9	1.1
Other	0.0	0.1	2.0	0.0	0.1	0.2
Corporate Tax Accruals	17.2	30.6	110.8	34.1	15.7	10.0
Federal Reserve Banks	0.2	3.5	22.9	0.4	1.8	2.1
Other	17.0	27.1	87.9	33.7	13.9	7.9
Indirect Business Taxes	8.9	19.2	61.7	17.7	9.8	5.5
Excise Taxes	8.2	15.7	37.3	16.3	8.0	3.4
Customs Duties	0.5	2.5	17.5	1.0	1.3	1.6
Other	0.1	1.1	6.8	0.2	0.6	0.6
Contributions for Social Insurance	6.3	52.9	446.7	12.5	27.1	40.2
Total	50.4	195.4	1112.0	100.0	100.0	100.0
Expenditures						
Purchases of Goods and Services	19.1	98.8	423.5	46.4	47.5	33.2
National Defense	14.3	76.8	312.9	34.7	37.0	24.5
Other	4.7	22.0	110.6	11.4	10.6	8.7
Transfer Payments	14.4	64.0	511.3	35.0	30.8	40.1
Grants-in-Aid to States and Local Governments	2.3	24.4	131.7	5.6	11.7	10.3
Net Interest Paid	4.4	14.4	186.5	10.7	6.9	14.6
Subsidies Less Current Surplus of Government Enterprises	1.0	6.5	22.8	2.4	3.1	1.8
Total	41.2	207.8	1275.9	100.0	100.0	100.0
Surplus or Deficit (−), NIPA	9.2	−12.4	−163.9			

benefits from social insurance funds (e.g., old age, survivors and disability insurance, hospital and supplementary medical insurance, unemployment insurance, federal employee retirement, railroad retirement, veterans benefits, food stamps, and a number of other small transfers). Another area that has been growing, now approximately 14.6 percent of expenditures, is interest on the federal debt, which has more than doubled as a percent of expenditures in the past 20 years. As government expenditures continue to grow faster than income, both debt and interest payments will increase. Finally, more than 10 percent of the budget goes to grants-in-aid to state and local governments.

STATE AND LOCAL RECEIPTS AND EXPENDITURES

The pattern of state and local government receipts and expenditures is shown in Figure 7.4. The solid and dotted lines suggest that, in contrast to federal experience, receipts were about equal to expenditures until about 1972 and have exceeded expenditures since then. The resulting surplus is indicated by the bars above the zero line at the bottom of the figure. However, about 16 percent of state and local receipts are in the form of grants-in-aid from the federal government. If these grants are excluded, state and local governments are running at a deficit, as indicated by the bars below the zero line at the bottom of the figure. It is interesting to note that the grants-in-aid in 1990 of $131.7 billion were about 80 percent of the federal deficit that year of $163.9 billion.[2]

[2]This does not mean that the grants-in-aid *caused* 80 percent of the federal deficit or that these grants should be discontinued. The figure is given to illustrate that, without this federal government help, state and local governments would also be running at a deficit or some state or local programs would have to be curtailed or canceled.

Figure 7.4. State and Local Receipts and Expenditures

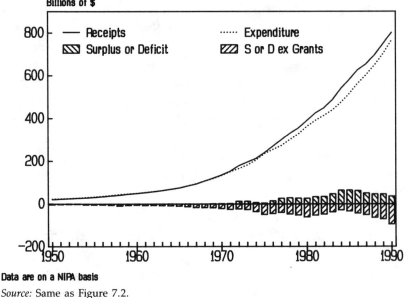

Data are on a NIPA basis

Source: Same as Figure 7.2.

Table 7.2 provides a more detailed picture of state and local receipts and expenditures for three years: 1950, 1970, and 1990. On the receipts side, the major source of revenues was indirect business taxes and nontax accruals, although this source has decreased from 69 percent to 47 percent of total revenues during this period. Within this area, the major percentage decrease has been in property taxes, which have fallen from 33 to 19 percent of revenues as taxing authorities have had to find other sources of revenue. Major increases in revenue have been from personal income taxes (i.e. 4 to 13 percent of revenues), other personal taxes (e.g., fees, fines, rents and royalties, and special assessments), and, as mentioned, federal grants-in-aid, from 11 to 16 percent.

On the expenditure side, the largest component is employee compensation, amounting to more than half of expendi-

Table 7.2.
State and Local Receipts and Expenditures—1950, 1970, and 1990

	1950	1970	1990	1950 Percent	1970 Percent	1990 Percent
		(Billions of Dollars)				
Receipts						
Personal Tax and Nontax Receipts	2.5	23.6	206.6	11.7	17.4	25.8
Income Taxes	0.8	10.9	106.2	3.8	8.0	13.3
Nontaxes	0.8	8.3	83.6	3.8	6.1	10.4
Other	0.9	4.4	16.6	4.2	3.2	2.1
Corporate Tax Accruals	0.8	3.7	24.2	3.8	2.7	3.0
Indirect Business Taxes	14.6	74.8	378.6	68.5	55.1	47.2
Sales Taxes	4.8	31.6	181.4	22.5	23.3	22.6
Property Taxes	7.1	36.7	150.1	33.3	27.0	18.7
Other	2.6	6.5	47.2	12.2	4.8	5.9
Contributions for Social Insurance	1.1	9.2	60.2	5.2	6.8	7.5
Federal Grants-in-Aid	2.3	24.4	131.7	10.8	18.0	16.4
Total	21.3	135.8	801.4	100.0	100.0	100.0
Expenditures						
Purchases of Goods and Services	19.8	119.4	674.3	88.0	89.1	88.1
Employee Compensation	10.1	71.1	400.9	44.9	53.1	52.4
Other	9.6	48.3	273.4	42.7	36.0	35.7
Transfer Payments	3.6	20.1	162.9	16.0	15.0	21.3
Net Interest Paid	0.1	-1.8	-41.6	0.4	-1.3	-5.4
Subsidies Less Current Surplus of Government Enterprises	-0.9	-3.6	-20.3	-4.0	-2.7	-2.7
Total	22.5	134.0	765.2	100.0	100.0	100.0
Surplus or Deficit (-), NIPA	-1.2	1.8	36.2			

tures. Another way to look at state and local spending is to review expenditures by function (not shown on the table). The major spending, by function, is for education (39 percent of total spending) and income support, social security, and welfare (15 percent of total).

THE FEDERAL DEFICITS AND DEBT

The federal government has run a deficit in most of the years since 1950. When income is less than outgo, the difference has to be borrowed. As a result, the federal debt has been growing. Figure 7.5 plots federal debt in billions of dollars from 1950 to 1990 and also shows this debt as a percent of GNP, the

Figure 7.5.   Federal Debt—Total and as a Percent of GNP

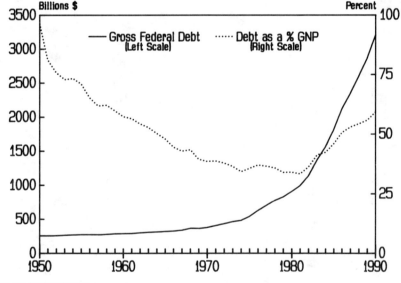

Data are for fiscal years

Source: ERP 1991, Table B-76, p. 375.

nation's output of goods and services. Although debt grew during most of this period, measured relative to the size of the economy is decreased to 33 percent of the nation's GNP in 1981. However, it grew to about 59 percent of GNP in 1990.

Is the Debt Really That Big?

It has been argued that the federal debt is not as great as it seems. For example:

> Not all federal debt is publicly held; as a matter of fact, about 25 percent is held in government trust funds such as the social security trust fund. Debt held by the government is an obligation the government owes to itself and should not be counted. However, as discussed later, these trust funds represent obligations that will ultimately have to be paid to someone;

> The federal government does not keep its books like a corporation would; the government just measures receipts and expenditures and does not distinguish between capital projects that will last for many years, and other types of expenditures. When a major project, such as a power plant, is built, the cost is charged to the years of construction, while a corporation would capitalize the asset and depreciate it over its expected life. In 1989, the government estimates that major public physical capital investment, both for defense and nondefense purposes, was about $129 billion, 2.4 percent of GNP; as indicated in Figure 7.2, total federal spending in 1990 was 23 percent of GNP;

> Federal government debt as a percent of GNP is not much different than that of many other major industrial nations.

These points may make the size of the deficit seem less, but it still continues to grow.

Financing the Federal Deficit

Financing the deficit is even more important than its size or growth. The federal debt makes major claims on the capital markets; it has also entailed borrowing overseas. Three major methods of financing the debt can be identified:

1. The first is either directly or indirectly out of the savings of individuals or corporations in the United States. If not purchased directly, government securities may be purchased indirectly through financial intermediaries such as banks, thrift institutions, and insurance companies. Funds used by the government are alternate uses of national savings; we, through our elected representatives, ultimately decide how these private savings are divided between the public and the private sector.

2. The second method is to obtain funds from abroad, which has become increasingly important. Foreign investors have been purchasing about 25 percent of new issues of U.S. government securities in recent years, and they now own about 15 percent of U.S. government debt. Consequently, their decisions to participate in regular Treasury financings, as well as their willingness to hold on to the securities they already own, can have a significant impact on U.S. security markets and interest rates. If they don't want U.S. securities, the funds will have to be raised in the United States somehow. The federal government has first claim on funds in the financial markets, because the money is needed to run the government and in-

ability to raise money would result in political and economic chaos. If the government's needs increase, other borrowers will either have to pay higher interest rates or will have to go without.

3. The final source of financing is for the Federal Reserve System to purchase these securities. This process is potentially inflationary, because, in effect, the Federal Reserve takes the bonds into its own portfolio and pays for the securities by crediting the Treasury's checking account for the proceeds. As the Treasury spends this money, it adds to the supply of money available to purchase the same amount of goods and services.

Reducing the Deficit

If the federal debt is such a problem, what can be done about it? The obvious answer is to reduce or eliminate the annual deficit and slow or halt the growth of the federal debt. But that is easier said than done, as repeated struggles by the Congress and the Administration in recent years amply indicate. Most of the easy cuts have been made in the budget. It is difficult to get agreement on increasing taxes in order to raise any significant amount of revenue; higher personal income taxes would be necessary, a politically unpalatable solution. Reducing spending is almost as difficult, as an examination of current spending patterns will show.

Review Table 7.1 again. Interest on the federal debt is untouchable, and as the debt grows interest payments will increase as a percent of federal outlays. Defense spending has been cut, and recent spending proposals indicate that certain programs will be reduced further. However, a good part of defense spending is for personnel, maintenance, procurement, and research and development. The 1990 to 1991 conflict in the

Middle East and the turmoil in the Soviet Union suggest that a significant "peace divided" will be very elusive. Running the legislative, executive, and judicial branches of the government takes less than 2 percent of the budget. Pensions, veterans' benefits, and items such as unemployment compensation are set by current law and are unlikely to be altered. The major items remaining are payments for social security, disability benefits, hospital and supplementary medical insurance. These are so large and so politically sensitive that they deserve some special discussion (see "How Does Social Security Work?" section). First, however, some comment is in order about the 1990 agreement to reduce the deficit.

A New Budget Process

As a result of long and difficult negotiations between the Administration and Congress at the end of 1990, a new and rather complex budget process has been established. Deficits no longer have fixed target ceilings each fiscal year, as was the case under the Gramm-Rudman law. The new system is more flexible in its approach to raising revenues and limiting spending. It does not guarantee to lower the budget deficit—but then Gramm-Rudman tried to and it didn't work. (In all the years of setting deficit ceilings under the Gramm-Rudman law, the deficit came in bigger than the target every year.)

Under the new procedure, three rules have been set:

1. Limits on *discretionary* spending;

2. Pay-as-you-go for *mandatory* spending; and

3. *Flexible* deficit targets.

Discretionary Spending.   Discretionary spending is spending controlled by annual appropriations. Discretionary spending is divided into three parts: defense, international, and domestic. International includes foreign economic and military aid, international financial programs, and operations of the Department of State. Defense includes the Department of Defense and other defense related activities such as the Department of Energy's nuclear weapons program. Domestic programs include running the executive, legislative, and judicial branches of government; science and space; environment; transportation; social services and education; housing; and veterans' medical care.

For the 1991 to 1993 fiscal years, caps are set for each of these three areas for budget authority (authority by law to incur financial obligations that will result in spending) and for outlays. For 1994 to 1995, discretionary spending as a whole has caps. These limits are adjusted periodically, particularly for changes in inflation rates. Outlays may exceed caps, but the budget authority caps may not be breached. Exceptions can be made, however, in an emergency designated as such by the President and Congress. For example, Operation Desert Storm in the Middle East was declared an emergency.

Mandatory Spending. Mandatory spending does not require annual appropriations and includes entitlements and other mandatory programs. Social security, Medicare, unemployment insurance, and pensions are considered mandatory programs.

With the two exceptions of social security and deposit insurance, changes in mandatory programs must be deficit neutral, i.e., they may not increase or decrease the deficit. They are on a *pay as you go* basis—increases in spending and receipts must offset each other in any one year. Again, these rules may be changed if an emergency is declared by Congress and the President.

Deposit insurance rules state that the amount needed to meet government deposit insurance commitments are not limited by the new process; spending to meet prior commitments is not limited in any way.

Social security has its own rules. Its receipts, spending, and trust funds are excluded from all calculations of a balanced budget. Social security, therefore, is not immune to a cut in payroll taxes, an increase in retirement benefits, or a shift in trust funds to other programs. The law, however, protects the social security trust funds by new Congressional rules that thwart consideration of legislation to reduce projected social security surpluses.

Deficit Targets. Although total deficit targets for future years are still set, they are flexible and nonbinding. However, many former skeptics believe that the new approach provides hope that progress will be made in making new programs pay for themselves. At least the new rules indicate that the seriousness of continuing large deficits is understood.

HOW DOES SOCIAL SECURITY WORK?

The social security trust fund is so large that it has its own rules; this major commitment of government to the public requires special discussion.

The social security system started in 1935 as a pension plan, with receipts to be held in trust for future beneficiaries just like in a corporate pension plan. However, the system quickly was changed to a pay as you go basis, with current workers' contributions paying for benefits to retirees. Gradually, very little relationship existed between the dollar amount contributed by a worker and the benefits received. Benefits were gradually extended to many who had not contributed, and since 1972 benefits have been increased each year by the increase in the consumer price index. (This practice is in sharp contrast to the private pension system, where cost-of-living increases are made infrequently and usually voluntarily by the companies concerned.) Although often considered as providing retirement benefits, the system also provides benefits for survivors of deceased participants as well as for participants who become disabled.

Social security and a part of Medicare are funded by payroll taxes paid equally by the employer and the employee, with the 1991 rate 15.3 percent up to an earnings ceiling of $53,400 a year. As indicated on Table 7.1, social security taxes now generate almost as much revenue as individual income taxes.

The increases made in social security benefits plus the annual adjustment in payments for inflation almost bankrupted the system. However, in 1983 the Greenspan Commission recommended increasing contributions, taxing a portion of the benefits to some recipients and gradually extending the retirement age to 67. These changes made the system solvent, and are also building reserves to ensure payment of benefits to present as well as future participants.

Medicare was introduced in 1966. It has two parts: hospital insurance (Part A), and supplementary medical insurance (Part B). The social security payroll tax is currently allocated between social security and Part A. When the hospital trust fund incurs a deficit, the allocation between the funds is changed to restore financial balance. Social security and Part A of Medicare project income and outgo 75 years ahead of the present. Part B, which makes projections only 3 years out, is financed about one-quarter from premiums paid by people eligible for benefits and three-quarters from general *tax* revenues. This drain on general tax revenues may explain why Medicare is a frequent target for Congressional action when ways of reducing the deficit are sought.

Figure 7.6 shows the income and outflow of the old-age and survivors insurance (social security) and disability insurance programs from 1965 through 1990. A slight surplus was

Figure 7.6.   OASI and DI Income and Outgo

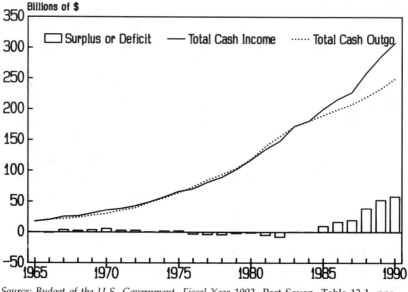

Source: *Budget of the U.S. Government, Fiscal Year 1992*, Part Seven, Table 13.1, pps. 165–171.

created prior to 1975, but the deficits thereafter created problems that were finally addressed in 1983. Since then, income has exceeded outgo, and beginning in 1985, a surplus has been created for the social security trust fund.

What is the outlook for this trust fund? Figure 7.7 indicates the projections for this fund, as contained in the 1989 annual report of the federal old-age and survivors insurance and disability insurance trust funds. As the figure indicates, a modest trust fund of about $157 billion at the end of 1989 will grow, under reasonable economic assumptions, to about $9.3 trillion by the year 2025. This apparently vast sum is an attractive target for various alternative spending schemes or for arguing that the payroll tax should be reduced.

However, under current law the fund would dwindle to zero by 2045. The reason for the swift decline is found in the

Figure 7.7.   Social Security Trust Fund Balance

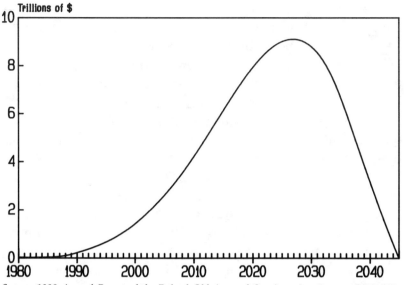

Source: 1990 Annual Report of the Federal Old-Age and Survivors Insurance and Disability
Insurance Trust Funds, Table F3, Alternative II-B, p. 135.

population mix. The baby boomers of the 1950s will be reaching
retirement age and the work force to support them by social
security contributions will be shrinking. In 1985, less than one-
fifth of the population was age 65 and over; by the year 2035
this will be more than one-third. As the retired population
increases and the work force shrinks, contributions to social
security will diminish, benefit payments will expand, and the
trust assets will be used up. A declining death rate will also
lengthen the payment to individuals already receiving benefits.

Social Security and the Federal Budget

The problem of Social Security running out of money is
even more complex. As social security payments are made into
the U.S. Treasury, they are invested exclusively in nonmarket-

able debt issued by the Treasury; the funds are then spent by the Treasury for general government purposes. In effect, the money received is spent and replaced in the trust fund by a Treasury IOU to be paid at a future time.

Interest is paid on this nonmarketable debt in the trust fund. As the assets of the fund grow, interest paid by the Treasury also grows as a percent of total income. In 1990 interest as a percent of income was about 5 percent; it will grow to 24 percent in 2020 and diminish thereafter. Understand that these interest payments are, in effect, a bookkeeping entry, a "wash" as far as total government income and outgo is concerned. Interest payments are an on-budget expense for the Treasury and interest received is off-budget income. A more realistic measure of a social security "surplus" is the annual difference between the public contributions and the payments to beneficiaries each year. In 1990 this difference amounted to about $46 billion, which will grow to about $130 billion in 2010 and by 2020 outgo will exceed income.

Thus, the social security trust fund is not some great pool of money available for beneficiary payments or for other programs. The current contributions from the public are spent by the government for general government purposes. The trust fund can be viewed as a segregated account on the government's books, reflecting the government's promise to pay future benefits as prescribed by law, by means of taxing or borrowing as funds are needed. The segregated trust fund makes clear the dimensions of this obligation and what will happen to this fund in the future under current law.

Proposals to use this trust fund for other purposes would merely transfer the IOUs to another program; future tax revenues or borrowing would still be required to pay for this alternative use. Proposals to reduce the social security payroll tax would just reduce Treasury receipts that are currently spent and reduce the growth of the pool of IOUs. The government's obligation to social security beneficiaries is set by current law and must be met (i.e., mandatory spending) unless the law is changed.

At some time in the next century the government will face the problem of social security benefit payments exceeding the income from payroll deductions. Some additional ways to cover benefit payments will have to be devised or benefits will have to be reduced. It might be well to start to address this issue now rather than later under the pressure of a perceived depletion of the trust fund.[3]

Other Trust Funds

Figure 7.8 indicates the status of the hospital insurance trust fund, Part A of Medicare. As mentioned earlier, this trust is funded by an allocation from monthly social security payroll deductions, and the contributions have been greater than the outgo since 1976.

Such is not true of Part B of Medicare, as shown in Figure 7.9. Approximately 25 percent of these expenses are paid for by contributions of beneficiaries and the remainder from general tax revenues. The fund has been constantly in deficit, and the deficits are growing. Expanded coverage, the soaring cost of medical benefits, and the greater use of medical services have created this problem. At some point, premiums will have to be increased or benefits reduced in order to reduce the drain on the Treasury.

[3]It has been proposed that the surplus of income over payments, instead of being invested in government securities, be lent to the private sector for investment. The interest income on the loans could assist in meeting future social security deficits. Such a development may make good sense economically but probably isn't politically feasible; it would be criticized as giving social security funds to corporations instead of using them to increase benefits.

Figure 7.8.   Hospital Insurance Income and Outgo

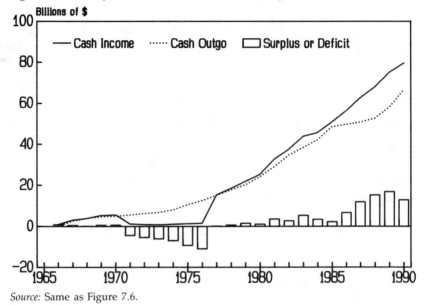

Source: Same as Figure 7.6.

Figure 7.9.   Medical Insurance Income and Outgo

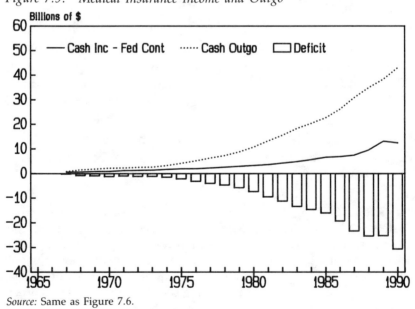

Source: Same as Figure 7.6.

SUMMARY

Unlike the private sector, monthly statistics are not readily available to monitor the performance of the government sector. Information on government purchases of goods and services is published as a part of the quarterly GNP reports and may be mentioned in the financial section of some newspapers. Details of total spending can be found in the Department of Commerce's monthly publication, the *Survey of Current Business.*

Most information about actions of the government is of a more qualitative nature and is covered in the general news sections of newspapers and other media. The figures, tables, and discussion in this chapter are intended to provide information on government income, outgo, and debt, so that activities reported in the media can be understood and interpreted with a somewhat better perspective.

Controlling federal spending is difficult. However, the new procedures adopted in October 1990 may reduce the size of the deficits in the next several years and slow the growth of the federal debt. A major long-term problem for the federal government is provision for payment of social security benefits as recipients grow and contributions from workers shrink. More immediate is the problem of Medicare, where three-quarters of the cost is not covered by payments from those who benefit.

CHAPTER 8

Interest Rates and Monetary Policy

In Chapter 1 interest rates were discussed briefly, indicating how movements in interest rates affect the decision-making process of the average person. The pattern of both short- and long-term interest rates from 1950 to 1990 was also reviewed, indicating how these rates were influenced by cyclical developments in the economy and changes in the inflation rate. Given this base of information, a closer look at interest rates can now be taken.

The day-to-day fluctuations in interest rates, like the day-to-day movements in the stock market, are generally random events that are impossible to predict. Over a period of time, however, the *trend* of interest rates does reflect the net results of certain forces pulling rates in different directions. Understanding and evaluating these forces should help make a reasonable estimate of the future pattern of rates, which should assist in making investment decisions.

This chapter discusses the following items:

Factors affecting interest rates, including the path of the economy, inflation, the financing needs of the federal government, international forces, the difficulties faced by U.S. financial institutions and, most importantly, the activities of the Federal Reserve;

Federal Reserve System is important in its influence on interest rate movements (a part of this chapter is devoted to its purpose, organization, and operations). The Federal Reserve operates through its influence on *bank reserves;* these are defined and discussed. Setting *monetary policy* is reviewed, followed by techniques used in monitoring the central bank;

The *level and pattern of interest* rates are also discussed. The *yield curve* as well as the different shapes it takes at different times in the business cycle is explained. Interest rate patterns of bonds of different maturity and quality are considered. Suggestions concerning what the average individual can expect to accomplish in anticipating changes in interest rates are also examined.

WHAT ARE INTEREST RATES?

Interest rates arise because people who don't have money and want it must pay something to those who have money and are willing to lend it for a reward, called *interest.* The *interest rate* is the amount received related to the amount lent, usually expressed as a percent computed by dividing the dollars of interest received per hundred dollars lent.

A distinction should be made between specific interest rates and interest rates in general. *Specific interest rates* on a particular financial instrument or type of instrument (e.g., a mortgage or a bank certificate of deposit) reflect the time for which the money is lent, the risk that the loan may not be repaid, and the current supply of and demand for funds available for lending in the marketplace.

Some specific rates, such as those on Treasury or corporate bonds, are set daily in dealer markets by negotiations between buyers and sellers, and are called *market rates*. Other rates, such as the *bank prime rate* (the interest rate banks charge their best customers) or the Federal Reserve *discount rate* (the rate at which banks can borrow from the Federal Reserve) are set by some group, and are called *administered rates*. However, these administered rates would not prevail for long if they did not reflect underlying market forces—ultimately they will reflect market rates.

These comments will initially focus on forces that affect the movement of interest rates generally rather than on rates of particular kinds of investments or their relationships with one another.

FACTORS AFFECTING INTEREST RATES

What are the major forces to watch in evaluating the future movement of interest rates? They include the economy, inflationary pressures, the federal government, international, the dollar, and U.S. financial institutions.

The Economy

Interest rates are strongly influenced by the expansion or contraction of the economy. When the economy is expanding, consumers have jobs and savings to lend, but also need to borrow for large purchases, such as a home or a car, or to finance other purchases by using credit cards. Business people need to borrow to build inventories or plants or to run their businesses generally as economic activity rises. As the demand for funds increases faster than the supply of savings grows, interest rates rise and act to ration the funds available. Of course, the opposite is also true; when the demand for funds is slack, interest rates fall.

Inflationary Pressures

Inflationary pressures also have an effect on interest rates, because the rates paid on most loans are fixed in the contract. A lender will be reluctant to lend funds for any period of time if the purchasing power of these funds will be less when they are returned. Consequently, the lender will demand a higher rate, a so-called inflationary premium, to lend money. Inflation pushes interest rates higher; deflation sends rates down.

Inflation pressures arise for a number of reasons, including the expansion of money and credit in excess of savings to support it, the purchase of federal debt by the banking system, or an increase in import prices (and indirectly domestic prices) because of a falling dollar.

The Federal Government

Another factor influencing interest rates is the actions of the nation's largest borrower, the federal government. Vast taxing powers of the federal government accords its debt the highest credit rating and therefore is a preferred investment. Its operation is vital to the country; the federal government has first claim on the funds available in the marketplace. With a budget of more than $1.4 trillion and an annual deficit projected at more than $300 billion, the financing of the annual deficit is equal to more than 15 percent of the total savings, foreign and domestic, available in the U.S. economy. Consequently, actions that affect the size of the deficit and the borrowing patterns of the Treasury have a very significant effect on interest rates.

INTERNATIONAL

International forces have exercised an increasingly important influence on U.S. interest rates. Several years ago, when U.S. interest rates were high relative to those of other major industrial countries, foreigners were eager to invest in the United States, which increased the supply of funds and exerted downward pressures on interest rates. To the extent that foreign investors are willing to lend funds to the United States, they supplement domestic sources of funds and push rates down. Should they decide to reduce their lending or, worse, sell their holdings to reinvest elsewhere in the world, funds needed in the United States would have to come from domestic sources, pushing rates up. Consequently, an important consideration for the Federal Reserve in setting monetary policy is whether U.S. rates are sufficiently high to maintain foreign interest in U.S. securities.

The Dollar

The dollar is the main currency in international trade and is used extensively in world markets. Orderly fluctuations of the dollar in foreign exchange markets are essential for domestic and international stability. Major or very volatile exchange rate movements in the dollar may force the Federal Reserve to intervene and may also affect U.S. monetary policy and interest rates.

U.S. Financial Institutions

Some of the major banks and thrift institutions are facing difficulties due to poor lending policies and a business contraction that has affected the ability of many borrowers to repay their bank loans. If any large institution is threatened with failure, it would not default on the funds owed to its depositors, as happened in the 1930s. Federal government actions would be taken to ensure the integrity of the deposits, regardless of the impact on the federal budget deficit. The Federal Reserve would make bank reserves available as necessary. This action would increase the supply of funds in the market. Initially interest rates would move down, but ultimately the increase in inflationary pressures would send rates higher. Changes in the health of the U.S. financial system have a significant effect on U.S. interest rates.

THE FEDERAL RESERVE SYSTEM

Probably the most important force to watch in evaluating future interest rate trends is the Federal Reserve. The Federal Reserve controls credit availability, for example, the *amount* of funds available to lend, and the *level of interest rates* at which this credit is made available. Its importance in the functioning of the financial system requires a longer discussion of the purpose, organization, and some of the responsibilities of the Federal Reserve.

Purpose

The Federal Reserve System was created by Congress in 1913 to provide for a safer, more flexible banking and monetary system. Over time, this original purpose has shifted to broader national economic and financial objectives:

Stability and growth of the economy;

A high level of employment;

Stability in the purchasing power of the dollar; and

Reasonable balance in transactions with foreign countries.

As the nation's central bank, the Federal Reserve contributes to the achievement of these broad objectives by its ability to influence money and credit in the economy.

The Federal Reserve is but one of the many forces that affect the economy. Other forces include federal government policies on taxes and spending (fiscal policy), wage and price policies of business, price shocks, policies of foreign countries, and changing expectations of businesses and consumers that affect their spending patterns. Nevertheless, the Federal Reserve exerts significant influence on the path of the economy.

Organization

The governing body of the Federal Reserve System is the Board of Governors, located in Washington, DC. The seven members of the Board are appointed for a 14-year term by the President, with confirmation by the Senate. The Chairman and Vice-Chairman are selected from Board members for four-year terms, also by the President with the confirmation of the Senate. The Board is not a part of the Administration. It is an independent agency of the federal government, although Congress can change its powers and duties by legislation.

The United States is divided into 12 Federal Reserve Districts, each with a district Federal Reserve Bank and its own president and directors. These banks have the duty of making recommendations to the Federal Reserve Board for changes in the *discount rate*, the interest rate which financial institutions must pay to borrow from the Federal Reserve. In addition, these banks hold the reserve balances for and make loans to depository institutions, furnish currency, collect and clear checks, and handle U.S. government debt and cash balances.

In addition to its responsibilities in regulating the supply of reserves in its efforts to influence economic activity, the Federal Reserve has other functions that should be mentioned briefly. The Federal Reserve acts for the government in foreign exchange markets, in close cooperation with the U.S. Treasury. In a world of flexible exchange rates, one of the objectives is to prevent disorderly conditions on exchange markets. The Federal Reserve also watches international developments, such as changes in interest rates overseas, in order to temper their effects on the U.S. economy.

The Federal Reserve also has supervisory and regulatory functions, which it shares with other federal banking agencies. The Federal Reserve supervises state-chartered banks that are members of the Federal Reserve System and all bank holding companies. (The Office of the Comptroller of the Currency supervises national banks, and the Federal Deposit Insurance Corporation (FDIC) supervises insured nonmember commercial banks and insured state-chartered savings banks.) The Federal Reserve also acts as the banker for the federal government, sets margin requirements for the purchase or carrying equity securities, and establishes and enforces rules that offer protection to consumers in financial operations. However, the most important function of the Federal Reserve is its control over banking reserves.

The members of the Federal Reserve Board are a part of the Federal Open Market Committee (FOMC). Other members of the FOMC are the President of the Federal Reserve Bank of New York and five other Reserve Bank presidents, who serve on a rotating basis. The FOMC directs the Federal Reserve's open market operations, the chief instrument of monetary policy, described in more detail later in this chapter. The FOMC meets formally eight times a year and more often if necessary.

Approximately one-third of the roughly 15,000 commercial banks in the United States belong to the Federal Reserve System. These member banks account for about 70 percent of the deposits of all commercial banks and about 40 percent of those of all depository institutions. National banks chartered by the federal government must belong to the system, and state banks may also be members. Since 1980, all depository institutions (commercial banks, foreign-related banking institutions, savings banks, savings and loan associations, and credit unions) are required to maintain reserves with the Federal Reserve System; they may also borrow from the Federal Reserve as necessary.

Member banks must subscribe to stock in the Reserve Bank of its district equal to 6 percent of its capital and surplus, 3 percent of which is paid in and the remainder subject to call by the Board of Governors. Owning this stock does not give member banks control of the policies of the Reserve Banks; however, member banks do receive a statutory dividend each year of 6 percent on the value of their paid-in stock. After paying expenses and the 6 percent dividend, the remaining earnings of the Federal Reserve, about 95 percent of the total, are turned over to the U.S. Treasury.

Reserves of Depository Institutions

The Federal Reserve influences overall monetary and credit conditions, and thus movements in the economy, through actions that affect both the *amount and cost of reserves* of depository institutions.

Reserves are defined by law as cash (currency and coin) held by depository institutions in their vaults plus the accounts of these institutions with their district reserve banks. Total reserves have two components. The first is *required reserves,* defined as the minimum percent of deposits the Federal Reserve requires a depository institution to hold (for most accounts, now 12 percent). Total reserves less required reserves are called *excess reserves.*

Reserves are provided in two forms. *Nonborrowed reserves* are obtained by depository institutions primarily from the Federal Reserve through Federal Reserve open market operations. *Borrowed reserves* are accomplished by a loan to the depository institution by the Federal Reserve. When borrowed reserves are subtracted from excess reserves, the balance is called *free reserves.* These reserve balances are reported weekly in financial newspapers as part of the consolidated balance sheet of the Federal Reserve Banks.

Another measure that is published together with the reserve information is called the *monetary base,* which includes currency held by the public and in the vaults of depository institutions plus reserves of depository institutions. Of the two components, currency comprises the larger, more than 80 percent. The monetary base, in effect, comprises the Federal Reserve's liability for currency in circulation and for reserve balances; it also represents monetary instruments that can function as reserves in the banking system. Some economists argue that the monetary base should be used as an operating target for monetary policy, but it is more generally used as an analytical device.

The fractional reserve system provides the Federal Reserve with a powerful tool to influence the amount of money and credit in the economy and thus the level of economic activity. If, for example, a reserve of 10 percent against deposits were required, every dollar of bank reserves held by the Federal Reserve would support ten times that amount in deposits in the banking system. For every dollar of excess reserves (reserves above those necessary to support the current level of deposits), the banking system can create new deposits and make loans to ten times the amount of excess reserves. (For example, on February 6, 1991, the Federal Reserve reported that total reserves equaled $61,190 billion and excess reserves $2,810 billion. Subtracting $161 million of bank borrowings from the Federal Reserve, free reserves equaled $2,649 billion, which could support additional bank lending of ten times that amount.) The Federal Reserve can significantly affect the ability of the banking system to expand or contract loans and deposits by taking action to increase or shrink reserves.

Influencing Reserve Positions

The Federal Reserve can affect the supply of reserves in three ways:

1. *Setting bank reserve requirements,* which is done by the Federal Reserve Board. Changing reserve requirements is considered a major step not often used. It affects all depository institutions and can have a significant impact on reducing or increasing funds available for lending.

2. *Discount lending.* Financial institutions may borrow from the Federal Reserve by pledging securities or loans they own, paying an interest rate called the *discount rate.* This rate is approved by the Board on the recommendation of the district Reserve Banks. Raising or lowering this rate can hinder or encourage borrowing and hence the supply of bank reserves. However, banks usually borrow from the Federal Reserve only for temporary or unusual reasons. Changes in the discount rate are more symbolic of the central bank's intentions than a major tool of monetary policy.

3. *Open market operations.* The most frequently used and most flexible tool of monetary policy is open market

operations, which are directed by the FOMC. When
the Federal Reserve sells U.S. Treasury securities out
of its portfolio to securities dealers, these dealers pay
for the securities with checks drawn on financial institutions; the Federal Reserve collects from these financial institutions by reducing their reserve accounts at
the Federal Reserve. This step reduces the lending
ability of financial institutions substantially more than
the amount of the payment because of the operations
of fractional reserves. When the Federal Reserve buys
securities and pays for them by crediting bank reserve
accounts, the opposite effect occurs. These actions
work indirectly on the economy through the supply
and the cost of funds, with a response lag that may
vary depending on the reserve position of the banking
system and the many other forces that influence the
economy.

Actions of the Federal Reserve are not the only factors that
cause changes in nonborrowed reserves. Currency in circulation reflects public demand for money and has a significant
seasonal pattern, for example, a big increase around holidays.
The Federal Reserve float—the difference between checks cred-
ited to bank reserve accounts but not yet collected from issuing
banks—is affected by random factors, such as storms or transportation strikes. Thus, Treasury and foreign official balances
at Federal Reserve Banks are very difficult to predict.

What the Federal Reserve Watches

What guides does the Federal Reserve use in determining
monetary policy? Prior to October 1979, the Federal Reserve
operated monetary policy by managing reserve positions to
achieve a certain level of the federal funds' rate. (*Federal funds*
are excess reserves that banks lend to each other for brief

periods, mostly overnight; the lending bank has excess reserves and the borrowing bank needs to cover a temporary reserve deficiency. The Federal Reserve actions impact reserve positions; therefore the federal funds' interest rate is the easiest to influence through open market operations.

In October 1979, this procedure was altered to focus on achievement of a certain growth rate in the money supply. Since late 1982, a more judgmental approach has been used, with the economic outlook, commodity prices, the monetary aggregates, interest rates, credit conditions, the foreign exchange position of the dollar, and other factors being considered.

Overall economic conditions are a primary focus of Federal Reserve analysis. In Chapters 2 through 8 a framework for such an analysis was provided. The Board has an exceptionally talented staff that analyzes available business and financial statistics to determine the current position and likely future path of the economy. In addition, the Board has an excellent intelligence network in the district banks, which submit regular reports on district conditions. These reports, contained in the so-called beige book, are usually summarized in the financial press.

The Money Supply

Another important monitoring tool is changes in the money supply. It is useful because it provides a clue to changes in the *amount* of money available to the public rather than the *cost* of this money. Several problems arise when the focus of monetary policy is on controlling changes in the money supply.

Before banking deregulation, a clear distinction could be made between funds held for transactions purposes and funds held as a store of wealth, or savings. Transactions accounts did not pay interest and were comprised of currency and demand deposit or checking accounts at banks. Savings accounts were interest-bearing deposits at banks and other savings institutions.

With deregulation, however, the picture has changed. Demand deposits may now pay interest. Checks can now be drawn against savings accounts; and the kinds of accounts have proliferated, including money-market mutual funds with checking privileges. Whether a deposit is for transactions or for savings is really in the mind of the owner of the account, which may change from time to time. The name or nature of the account is of little help.

As a result, measures of the money supply have had to be expanded, and long-time historical relationships reconsidered. The definitions of the money supply now include the following:

1. *M1* includes balances (currency, travelers checks, demand deposits, and interest-bearing accounts with unlimited checking authority) that are commonly used for transactions purposes to purchase goods and services;

2. *M2* includes M1 plus liquid assets whose nominal values are fixed and can be converted into transactions balances with relative ease, for example, money-market accounts, time and savings deposits, and money-market mutual funds;

3. *M3* includes both M1 and M2 as well as liquid assets held by large asset holders, for example, $100,000 or more.

Statistical analysis indicates that, in the long run, prices in the economy will rise in proportion to the rise in the money supply. M2, among the aggregates, is the measure that most closely conforms to movements in GNP in current dollars. This relationship implies that the Federal Reserve can control the trend in nominal GNP by controlling M2, which is why many economists emphasize the use of this measure to establish and monitor monetary policy.

However, several difficulties are encountered in using the money supply for this purpose. The first is the blurring of the distinction between money used for *transaction balances* and for a *store of wealth*. The transaction balances are those involved in attempting to control economic activity. The second is the difficulty in identifying changes in the trend of money supply movements, determining the lead time between these turning points and then the subsequent impact on business. It is one thing to look at a chart of historical movements in the money supply and business activity; it is another to pick turning points contemporaneously as these lines jiggle up and down. The final problem is that money has not only quantity but also velocity, that is, the rapidity with which it changes hands varies.

For all these reasons, many economists question the utility of using the money supply as the principal tool in setting monetary policy, regardless of the theoretical basis for its use. However, it is a useful measure to watch in anticipating changes in Federal Reserve policy.

Watching the Federal Reserve

Officials at the Federal Reserve tend not to indicate plainly what their intentions are with respect to monetary policy; these must be determined by watching what they watch and watching what they do. As indicated earlier, they watch business conditions; an average individual can do this as well. Granted the economists at the Federal Reserve have many and more sophisticated tools at their disposal, but understanding the strength or weakness of the economy and anticipating major turning points are well within the abilities of the average individual willing to take a little time to develop a perspective of what is going on.

Clues as to what the Federal Reserve is going to do can be obtained by watching movements in the money supply, changes in bank reserve positions, and changes in the federal funds rate. Another clue is to watch the speeches and statements of Federal Reserve officials. The Chairman is required to testify before Congress twice a year (February and July) on the Federal Reserve's assessment of the economy, credit conditions and their projected growth rates of the money supply for the year ahead. In addition, the minutes of the FOMC are reported in the press. Unfortunately the release is made about 45 days after each meeting, considerably reducing their usefulness. In addition, members of the Board often make speeches that touch on their views of monetary policy, and these speeches are reported in the financial press.

One way of watching the Federal Reserve's actions is to monitor changes in the federal funds rate and the discount rate. Figure 8.1 plots the monthly movements of these rates from January 1987 through early 1991. The upward movement in the funds rate through early 1989 raised the cost of borrowed funds, clearly indicating the concern of the FOMC with inflationary conditions. This concern gradually abated through the fall of 1990. The worry became the weakness of the economy, which was very evident in late 1990. Policy was eased quickly, as indicated by the sharp fall in both the funds rate and quick cuts in the discount rate. Interest rates generally, especially short-term rates, fell rapidly.

Another method of watching the Federal Reserve's actions is to plot the dollar value of the M2 money supply and match its movements against growth targets the Federal Reserve has made public in the Chairman's Congressional testimony each February (reviewed again in July). Figure 8.2 presents this information for 1989 through early 1991. As the figure indicates, money supply growth lagged behind the target range

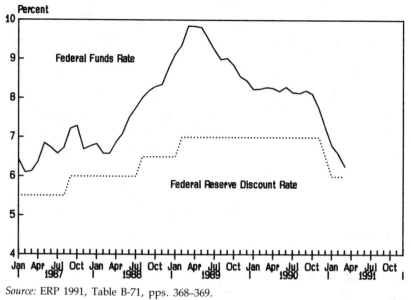

Figure 8.1.   Federal Funds and the Discount Rate

Source: ERP 1991, Table B-71, pps. 368–369.

Figure 8.2.   M2 Money Supply, 1989–91

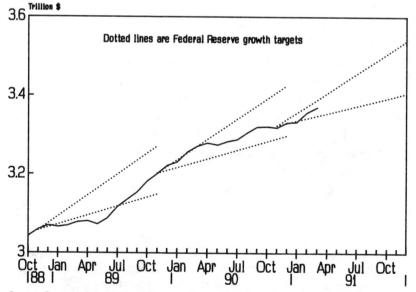

Source: Current data: Federal Reserve Data, *Wall Street Journal*, every Friday; earlier data, SCB, February 1991, p. S-15; ERP 1991, Table B-67, p. 363; target ranges from *Federal Reserve Bulletin*, March 1991, Table 1, p. 148.

through the first half of 1989, but then grew to the top of the new range in early 1990. Growth thereafter was sluggish, and, in fact, during most of this period the central bank was more preoccupied with controlling the funds' rate than the money supply. However, the very sluggish money supply growth in the fall of 1990 and early 1991 drew attention to the money supply again, and it recently has become a useful indicator to monitor Federal Reserve activity.

INTEREST RATES

In Chapter 1, interest rates were briefly mentioned, indicating that short-term interest rates (i.e., the rates on money lent for short periods of time) are more volatile than long-term interest rates. The pattern of interest rates during most of the postwar period was also reviewed, finding that these rates were responsive to cyclical movements in the economy and also had long trends that were related to movements in the inflation rate. Some additional characteristics of interest rate movements need to be added.[1]

In addition, to the level of interest rates (covered in Chapter 1) two other characteristics of interest rates are worth understanding. The first is changes in the so-called *yield curve*, which refers to the relationship among yields of securities with different maturities. The second characteristic is *yield spreads*, which refers to the relationships among bonds of different maturity or quality.

[1]This discussion will be confined to interest rates. Information about the bond market and bond portfolio management will be found in a companion volume written by the staff of the New York Institute of Finance, *How the Bond Market Works* (New York Institute of Finance, 1988).

The Yield Curve

The interest payment on a fixed-income security relative to its current market price provides a measure of the security's yield. The yield curve reflects the structure at a point in time of the yields of various fixed-income securities of the same quality (usually U.S. government securities) as the maturity lengthens from short- to intermediate- to long-time periods to maturity. An example is shown in Figure 8.3, which is a snapshot of the yields on U.S. Treasury securities of various maturities on February 12, 1991. (The data are plotted by calendar quarters in order to include more securities with short maturities). At that time, 3 month Treasury bills were yielding about 6 percent, and the yield on longer-term Treasury securities gradually rose to just under 8 percent at 30 years.

Figure 8.3.   Yield Curve, February 13, 1991

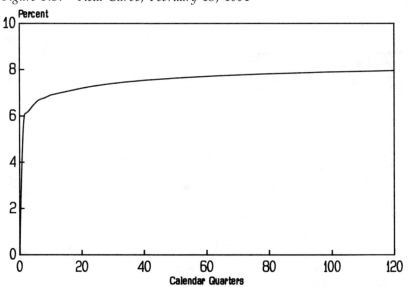

Source: Prices from *Wall Street Journal,* "Treasury Bonds, Notes and Bills," February 13, 1991.

The shape of the curve will change each day, reflecting both changes in the level of interest rates generally and changes in the shape or the slope of the curve as the yields for securities of particular maturities reflect price movements at different rates.

How Does the Yield Curve Change?　Financial economists generally identify three broadly defined shapes of the yield curve, with the shape moving from one kind to another over time:

> *Upward sloping,* a shape that has prevailed most of the time in recent years, when the yield on short-term maturity securities has been lower than that of long-term securities, so that the slope of the curve is upward. (See Figure 8.4.) Such a pattern of yields prevails most of time, as investors demand a higher interest payment for waiting longer for the return of the principal they have lent;

Figure 8.4.　Downward Sloping Yield Curve

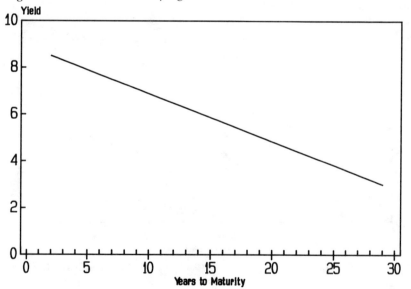

Downward sloping, a pattern that occurs less frequently and often lasts for short periods. In this case, short-term securities have a higher yield than securities with a longer maturity and the curve slopes downward (See Figure 8.5.);

Relatively flat, indicating that yields are roughly the same at all maturities, as investors appear indifferent to the length of the time they wait for repayment of the principal of their investment.

Why Does the Slope Change? The level of yields basically reflects the supply and demand for funds. The shape of the yield curve is influenced by two factors: expectations, of borrowers and lenders, about the future path of interest rates, and the monetary policy of the Federal Reserve.

Reflect for a moment on the attitudes of both lenders and borrowers if they expect interest rates to rise considerably in

Figure 8.5. Upward Sloping Yield Curve

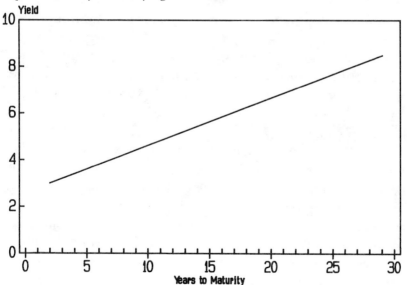

the future. Lenders will prefer shorter maturity investments, which will fall less in price as rates rise, and anticipate better buying opportunities later. Borrowers, however, will prefer longer maturity investments so that they can lock up current low rates in order not to have to pay higher interest later. With the downward pressure on short rates as lenders provide short-term funds and upward pressure on long rates as borrowers try to lock in prevailing rates, the yield curve slopes upward. The reverse is also true; the yield curve has a downward slope when interest rates are expected to fall significantly, as lenders seek to lock in higher long rates and borrowers seek short maturities that can be extended at a later date.

The Federal Reserve can also affect the yield curve as it alters monetary policy. The Federal Reserve usually confines its open market operations to shorter maturity securities; the economic effects and the reflection of monetary policy in long rates takes a little longer.

The Yield Curve and Business Cycles.   As a generalization, an upward sloping yield curve is steepest at the trough of a business cycle. At the trough, interest rates are expected to rise in the future and borrowers are beginning to increase their activity, thus demanding long-term funds and trying to get rates as low as possible. Lenders, however, prefer to supply funds for short periods of time because they expect to get higher rates later.

As the economy expands, interest rates move up; either because of increasing demand for funds or, as the economy nears full employment, the Federal Reserve tightens monetary policy, pushing interest rates up in order to slow the economy and control inflation. As rates move up, investors' and borrowers' expectations of the future level of interest rates change; they become less concerned about the time to maturity of a loan and the yield curve flattens.

Toward the peak of a cycle, when lower rates can be anticipated at some future time when the economy contracts, the upward pressures on the short end of the market intensify; lenders are more willing to supply long-term funds while borrowers have a greater interest in short-term borrowing. Moreover, monetary policy is at its tightest toward the end of the cycle. Consequently, short rates go up more than long rates, and the yield curve often becomes "inverted," with short rates becoming higher than long rates.

In past business cycles, an inverted yield curve has preceded a contraction in business activity, with the lead time from the inversion to the business cycle peak varying from five to seven quarters. The level of all interest rates, however, usually does not turn down until the cycle itself has peaked.

With respect to recent conditions, the yield curve was slightly inverted in mid-1989, and the peak of the present cycle probably was in mid-1990. Interest rates generally began to decline in the fall of 1990.

Bond Maturity Spreads

Another way of examining differences in bonds is to measure the spread or *yield difference between bonds of the same quality but of different maturities*. Figure 8.6 shows the monthly yields of three-month Treasury bills compared with the yields of ten-year Treasury notes (the two lines at the top of the figure) and then the difference in percentage points between the two (the solid line at the bottom of the chart). U.S. Treasury securities are used because they are of the highest quality, and price movements therefore reflect only maturity differences.

The movement of the bottom line indicates that the shape of the yield curve changes over time. From early 1988 to the spring of 1989 the Federal Reserve maintained a tight monetary policy in an effort to slow a rising economy and contain inflation. This policy was effective, and a sluggish economy became a more important concern of the Federal Reserve; the federal funds rate peaked in March, as shown in Figure 8.1.

As short rates moved up in 1988 to 1989, the yield on the longer maturity issue remained relatively flat, so that the yield curve flattened, as typically happens as the peak of a business cycle approaches. (See Figure 8.6.) Yield spreads continued to fall, and an inversion of the yield curve almost occurred in June 1989. Thereafter, short rates fell more than long rates, and the yield curve became more upward sloping. An investor who understands these yield shifts between short- and long-maturity securities, and correctly anticipates major turning points in interest rates can improve investment performance by shifts between securities with different maturities.

Figure 8.6.   Bond Maturity Yield Spreads, 1987–91

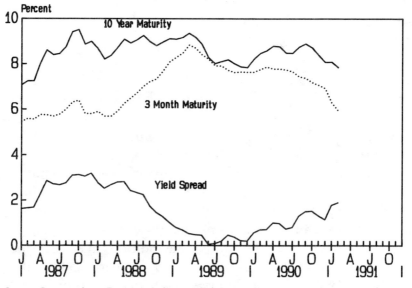

Source: Current data: *Economic Indicators,* February 1991, p. 30; earlier data, ERP 1991, Table B-71, p. 368.

Figure 8.7.   Bond Quality Yield Spreads, 1987–91

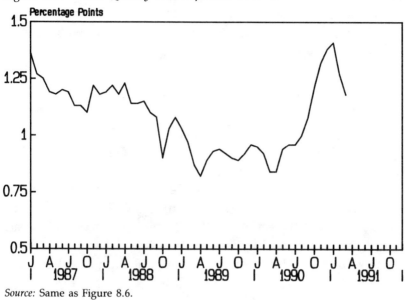

Source: Same as Figure 8.6.

Bond Quality Spreads

Another interesting shift in interest rates occurs in the *yield differentials between bonds of different quality.* Figure 8.7 plots the monthly yield difference between corporate bonds of the highest quality (Aaa rating) and those of the lowest investment quality (Baa).[2] Just as investors shift their preferences in maturities, they also shift their interest in issues of different quality.

As the economy expands, investors are more confident of the ability of corporations to maintain payments on their bonds, and bonds of lower quality but higher yield are in greater demand. Thus, the spread between high- and low-

[2]Bond ratings range from Aaa, the highest quality, through Aa, A and Baa. Bonds rated Ba and below are not considered of investment grade, and are often referred to as either *high yield* or *junk* bonds.

quality issues narrows. Of course, the opposite is true as investors anticipate a business contraction. Figure 8.7 indicates the narrowing of yields until early 1989 and the widening of spreads thereafter.[3]

SUMMARY

This chapter provided an overview of interest rates and the factors that influence their movements. Particular attention was paid to the operations of the Federal Reserve System and the relationship of fixed-income securities with various characteristics. Following actions of the Federal Reserve can be accomplished by careful reading of the financial section of leading newspapers. However, a good rule of thumb is that shifts in Federal Reserve policy are predicted about ten times more often than actually occur.

Interest rate movements are often charted in the financial media, especially the *Wall Street Journal.* Financial publications are available from the Federal Reserve Board and the district banks that provide data on interest rates. Moreover, as even a casual glance at the financial press will indicate, commentaries on Federal Reserve policy are legion.

It is not the purpose of this chapter to assist an investor in managing a bond portfolio. This is a highly skilled task best left to experts. However, we have tried to provide some guidance

[3]Other differences among bonds are routinely considered by investors in managing bond portfolios, such as the tax status of the bond, the coupon rate, and the ability of the issuer to call the bond for refunding before maturity. These factors are beyond the scope of this book; explanations can be found in books on bond portfolio management (e.g., H. Gifford Fong, "Portfolio Construction: Fixed Income" in *Managing Investment Portfolios,* 2nd ed., John L. Maginn and Donald L. Tuttle, eds., Warren, Gorham & Lamont, 1990).

for the many decisions an individual must make that require some knowledge of interest rate movements. Trying to call short-term fluctuations in interest rates, however, is nearly as difficult as calling short-term movements in stock prices. The financial press often publishes surveys of economists' predictions of interest rates in detail by calendar quarters a year or more ahead. Some forecasts are, at best, a triumph of optimism over reality. Nevertheless, one who follows the economy and financial markets reasonably closely should be able to determine the following factors about interest rates, with increasing degrees of difficulty and uncertainty:

1. The current *trend* of interest rates, either up or down;

2. Whether a significant *turning point* in rates has occurred, preferably within a short time after the turning point; and

3. The *extent of the expected movement* in rates, or at least identifying the factors that will determine the extent of the change.

Given the many forces acting on rates, however, it is almost impossible to predict other factors.

CHAPTER 9

Economic Trends and Cycles

Understanding the monthly movements in the economy is easier if they are examined in a broader perspective of the past and potential real growth of the economy, the prospects for inflation, and the present phase of the business cycle. This chapter provides the following background information to provide this perspective:

Judgments about long-term economic growth rates are made by estimating the future size of the *labor input* and the *productivity* of that input. Two government bodies have studied this issue and concluded that economic growth between 2 and 3 percent per year in real GNP is a reasonable range to use for the next five years;

A review of the pattern of prices in the United States since the Civil War reveals an upward sweep of prices after World War II, suggesting that an *inflationary bias* may now be built in the U.S. economy. A review of forces that will push prices up as well as down suggests that inflation rates between 4 and 6 percent are likely in the years ahead;

Business cycles are periods of expansion and contraction characteristic of nations that organize their work through private business enterprises. They vary in their length and severity, and no two cycles are alike. Certain repetitive characteristics have been identified, but no single explanation for cycles has been determined. One method of tracking cycles is by following groups of time series called *economic indicators* that have historically led, coincided with, or lagged cycle turning points.

ESTIMATING FUTURE ECONOMIC GROWTH[1]

A carefully watched statistical measure of the health of the economy is the annualized growth rate of inflation-adjusted or "real" GNP. Each month the Department of Commerce estimates the annualized growth rate for the most recent calendar quarter. Each July data are revised for the previous three years, and periodically revisions are made for longer time periods. Economists for both public and private organizations make

---

[1]The comments in this section are based on an excellent article by C. Alan Gardner, "How Fast Can the U.S. Economy Grow," in the *Economic Review*, Federal Reserve Bank of Kansas City (December 1989). pp 3–23.

estimates of growth rates for future years. Yet little is said about how fast this growth should or could be.

Potential Output

How fast the economy *should* grow is important for government decisions about fiscal and monetary policy. An especially fast growth rate can cause increased demand that cannot be satisfied by the current supply of labor and industrial capacity, leading to higher inflation. A sluggish growth rate causes lost output of goods and services and higher unemployment. Economic policy attempts to modify growth rates in order to achieve balanced output and price stability.

Knowing how fast the economy *could* grow, that is, its *potential output*, permits a more intelligent interpretation of past or projected growth rates. Potential output may vary from actual output for many months because of cyclical variations in the economy. (See Figure 9.10) Real output exceeded potential in 1964 to 1969 and 1972 to 1973 periods, but fell below in 1974 to 1976 and 1980 to 1987. During 1988 to 1989 the economy was operating close to its potential, but in 1990 was below potential once again.

The concept of potential output is important because it provides a benchmark against which policymakers can evaluate the economy's actual performance and determine what actions, if any, are necessary to modify the pace of activity. Understanding where the economy is with respect to potential enables the observer of the economy to anticipate and evaluate policy changes.

In estimating potential output, a somewhat different approach is used in contrast with the estimates of GNP that reflect the demand for goods and services and how they are taken off the market by consumers, business, government, and net exports. Instead, the potential is measured by *labor input* (the employed civilian labor force multiplied by the number of hours worked per year) and the *productivity* (or real output per hour) of that input.

Trends in Potential Output

The long-term trend of potential real output in the United States has been upward because of the growth in labor input and improvements in labor productivity: however, this rate of growth has slowed. The Congressional Budget Office has estimated that potential real output fell from an annual growth rate of 3.7 percent in 1960 to 1969 to 3.1 percent in 1970 to 1979 and 2.6 percent in 1980 to 1990. Diminishing productivity growth has been the primary cause of this slowing.

Figure 9.1 presents these estimates of potential prepared by the Congressional Budget Office and compares them with

Figure 9.1.   Actual and Potential Real Output 1954–90

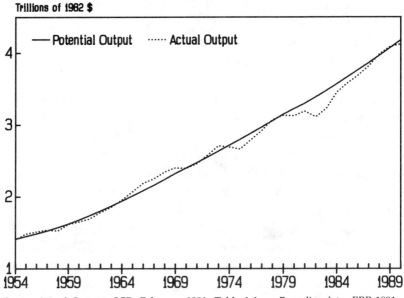

Trillions of 1982 $

Source: Actual Output: SCB, February 1991, Table 1.1, p. 7; earlier data, ERP 1991, Table B-1, p. 286; potential output direct from Congressional Budget Office.

actual output. In this instance, the output measure is not GNP but rather gross domestic product (GDP) in constant 1982 dollars. GDP measures output by factors of production in the United States only and excludes income from abroad. The movement of the dotted line, actual output, above and below the solid line, potential output, reflects the variations mentioned earlier.

What about future potential growth? Estimating future economic growth requires estimating changes in the labor input and changes in labor productivity. Labor input depends on growth of the labor force and to a lesser extent the number of hours worked per worker each year. Changes in productivity depend on improvements in the quality of labor as well as increases in the quantity and quality of capital (the tools and equipment that labor uses).

Labor Force Trends

The labor force grew at a high 2.7 percent annual rate in the 1970s, but growth slowed to a 1.7 percent rate in the 1980s. The postwar baby boom began entering the labor force in the 1960s, with the peak effect in the 1970s. An increasing number of women also entered the labor force in the 1970s and the 1980s, reaching 57 percent of the labor force in the period 1988 to 1989. The number of young people entering the labor force will slow in the next five years, reflecting the sharp drop in the birth rate in the late 1960s and early 1970s. Moreover, the percent of women in the labor force is unlikely to increase much further. Consequently, labor input should grow only about 1 percent a year until the end of the decade, and little change is expected in the number of hours worked.

Productivity Trends

What about the outlook for the factors affecting productivity? Improvement in labor quality declined in the 1970s and

1980s. Part of this decline was due to the lower experience level of the labor force, because the younger workers and the women entering the labor force had less experience than older workers. Another factor sometimes mentioned is a decline in the educational attainment of the labor force.

As for the quantity of capital, net investment spending (total investment spending less the depreciation of existing capital stock) slowed in the United States in the 1970s; and even more so in the 1980s. Several reasons for this slowing in investment have been suggested. Import competition discouraged investment in plant and equipment. The national savings rate has been low, and heavy credit demands (both private and public) kept interest rates (adjusted for inflation) high by historical standards. Some investment (e.g., spending necessary for pollution control) does not increase capacity. The big jump in oil prices in the 1970s made a good deal of capital equipment obsolete. And technological progress, which affects the quality of capital input, also slowed in the 1970s as research and development expenditures declined as a percent of national output.

Some factors will affect productivity favorably in the next five years. The experience level of the labor force will increase. Net investment spending will rise as an improvement in the trade balance increases demand for U.S. products overseas. Firms are spending more on equipment and less on structures, increasing capital efficiency. An older labor force will save more, making more funds available for investment. American industry has been forced by competition, both domestic and foreign, to become more efficient. Another factor is the possibility of smaller federal budget deficits, which would release more funds for private investment.

Several different estimates of potential output have been made. In January 1990 and again in 1991, the Congressional Budget Office estimated that potential GNP will grow on average about 2¼ percent per year over the next five years. The

President's Council of Economic Advisers estimates the potential growth rate at about 3 percent. The primary differences are assumptions about future gains in productivity. A reasonable approach is to assume growth somewhere between 2 and 3 percent annually. This range can be used to evaluate quarterly and annual growth rates, actual and projected, in the period ahead.

INFLATION

Chapter 3 touched briefly on inflation, the inequities it causes, and the various ways price changes are measured. In this section the outlook for inflation in the next several years is examined. Such an outlook is important in evaluating economic policies and the economic outlook, and is critical in making investment decisions.

Figure 9.2 provides a very long perspective on the level of prices in the United States, showing an annual consumer price index (CPI) from the Civil War to 1990. The figure indicates the very moderate increases in prices prior to the end of World War II. Two periods of rising prices are evident—just after the Civil War and during the 1920s—but they were followed by periods of price declines. However, prices increased significantly after World War II.

Another way to look at the price changes is as follows: Prices doubled from 1860 to 1945, a period of 85 years; they doubled again in the next 24 years, 1946 to 1969; they doubled again in the next 10 years from 1970 to 1979, and they almost doubled again in the 10 years from 1980 to 1990. These numbers suggest that the U.S. economy may have a long-term inflationary bias.

Figure 3.3 showed the December-to-December changes in the CPI from 1950 to 1990, and Figure 3.1 plotted the CPI less food and energy prices. Figure 9.3 plots these two prices in-

Figure 9.2.   Consumer Price Index 1860–1990

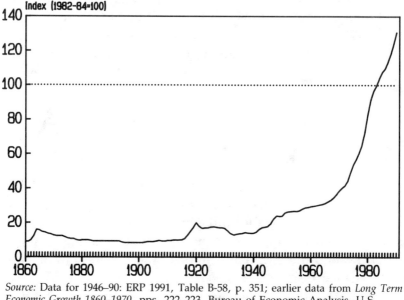

Source: Data for 1946–90: ERP 1991, Table B-58, p. 351; earlier data from *Long Term Economic Growth 1860–1970*, pps. 222–223, Bureau of Economic Analysis, U.S. Department of Commerce, Washington, D.C., June 1973. Computations by the author.

dexes on the same chart for the 1958 to 1990 period. (Data for 1950 to 1957 are not available for the CPI less the food and energy components.)

The two price series track each other reasonably well, with the CPI more volatile because of greater fluctuations in food and energy prices. Food price fluctuations can be blamed on the weather and are random events that ordinarily correct themselves. Energy prices are a different matter. While energy prices can be removed from price indexes, it does not eliminate the secondary effects as higher energy costs get embedded in the prices of products that use energy in production. Such effects can be seen in the price changes in 1974 and again in 1980 to 1981.

Figure 9.3.   CPI With and Without Food and Energy Prices

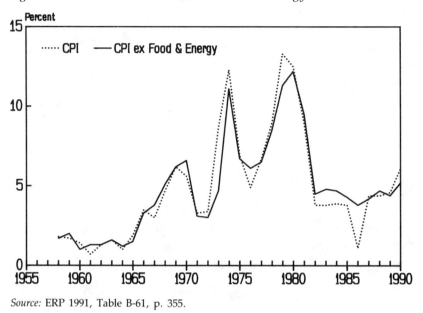

Source: ERP 1991, Table B-61, p. 355.

The average price increase for both series is the same, 4.85 percent for the 1958 to 1990 period. However, if the two series are averaged for subperiods, the results are different (see Table 9.1).

In Table 9.1, the first period, 1958 to 1965, the average change in the two series was about the same. However, in the 1966 to 1981 period, the inclusion of energy prices caused the CPI to increase faster than did the index without food and energy. In the more recent period, when oil price changes were more subdued, the CPI moved up less. The index without the volatile components of food and energy is often referred to as the *core inflation rate,* and the 4.5 percent average rate in the past nine years is disturbing and a cause of considerable concern to the Federal Reserve.

Table 9.1.
Average Annual Percent Changes, CPI and CPI Excluding
Food and Energy

	CPI	CPI Excluding Food and Energy
1958 to 1965	1.43	1.45
1966 to 1981	7.06	6.73
1982 to 1990	3.99	4.51

Future Price Expectations

With this background, what is the inflation rate, as measured by the CPI, likely to be over the next five years or so? Are we in for a period of deflation, as some economists predict? Or are forces building that may lead to a period of high inflation?

Oil Prices. When examining the forces that may push prices up, oil prices are a good place to start. Prior to the summer of 1990, oil prices tumbled. Overproduction and price cutting by OPEC (Organization of Petroleum Exporting Countries), increased production from new sources, lower world demand due to sluggish economic growth, and more efficient energy use pulled prices down to between $15 and $18 a barrel. Prices jumped quickly when Iraq invaded Kuwait, and the threat of losing a substantial portion of Middle East supply drove prices up to $40 a barrel, with higher prices predicted. With the successful military action of the Coalition forces, the threat of Iraqi domination of oil supplies was significantly reduced. Meanwhile other oil producers stepped up production, so that supplies quickly regained their prewar level and prices fell back to under $20 a barrel again.

This recital of events indicates one thing: Supply is ample but very unstable. OPEC supplies more than 40 percent of the world demand for oil, and the political turmoil of that area was demonstrated clearly by the invasion of Kuwait and its aftermath. Should some unpredictable event cut off OPEC oil or severely restrict its availability, alternative sources could not make up the loss and higher oil prices would be inevitable.

The Dollar. Chapter 6 discussed the decline in the dollar relative to other major currencies. The dollar's decline causes increases in import prices as foreign producers charge more dollars for their products to avoid losses when they convert dollars into their own currencies. Initially they may accept lower profit margins to maintain market share, but this policy has limits. When foreign producers raise their prices, experience indicates that U.S. producers raise their prices also instead of trying to increase their market share.

A lower dollar also makes investment in the United States less attractive to overseas investors—they have been major purchasers of U.S. Treasury bonds issued to finance the federal deficit. A change in attitudes about the attractiveness of U.S. investment would force these funds to be raised in the United States, forcing U.S. interest rates up. Higher U.S. interest rates either curtail U.S. demands for funds or lead to higher prices to offset higher costs.

Compensation. Another potential inflationary force is the erosion of real employee compensation in the United States; in almost half the years since 1975, the increase in compensation has been less than the inflation rate. Figure 9.4 plots the annual increase or decrease in real hourly compensation (hourly compensation less the CPI each year) from 1950 through 1990. The deterioration in real earnings since 1975 is evident. While this deterioration may not be reversed during 1990 to 1991, it is unlikely that workers will accept lower living standards indefinitely. Higher wages will lead to higher prices.

The Federal Deficit. Chapter 7 discussed the federal deficit and the inflationary implications of how it is financed. Deficits financed through the banking system are inflationary.

Figure 9.4.   Annual Change in Real Compensation Per Hour

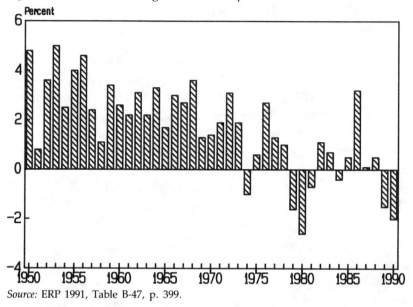

Source: ERP 1991, Table B-47, p. 399.

Outlook.   Does this review of inflation forces lead to the conclusion that another bout of double-digit inflation lies ahead? Some offsetting forces are at work; for example, progress may be made on controlling the federal deficit. The anti-inflationary bias and the firm response of the Federal Reserve to inflationary forces are well-known. However, as in the fall of 1990, when a business contraction is under way, economic stimulation can become a more important priority to the Federal Reserve than fighting inflation.

The critical question is whether the American people would tolerate another 1980 to 1983 period of tight money to wring inflation out of the system, and whether, from a longer-term point of view, they will be willing to accept budget cuts in entitlement programs that are politically popular.

A reasonable conclusion is that an inflationary bias is built into the U.S. economy. While a return to double-digit inflation rates is not considered likely, neither is inflation falling to a 3 to 4 percent range. A more likely range is 4 to 6 percent, with occasional bursts outside that range. If this conclusion is correct, inflation protection should be a part of all business and investment plans.

BUSINESS CYCLES

Business cycles are periods of *expansion* and *contraction* in aggregate economic activity found in nations that organize their work mainly in private business enterprises.[2]

Business cycles vary in how long they last, how high or low the economy moves during the cycle, and how broadly the economy is affected. In the United States, peacetime expansions have averaged about 1.5 to 3 years, contractions have averaged about 1 to 2 years, and the total cycle about 2.5 to 5 years. Considerable deviations around these averages have occurred, and each cycle has its own particular characteristics. However, business-cycle expansions generally have been longer and contractions much shorter after World War II than before, and the contractions have been less severe.

Several explanations have been offered for this development. Spending for services has increased, and such spending does not vary much during a cycle. (Examples are housing costs, household maintenance, and medical care, which account for almost two-thirds of consumer spending for ser-

[2]*Contraction* is a better word to describe the downside part of a business cycle than *recession*. Recession was a political euphemism invented in 1938 to avoid calling the contraction at that time a *depression*, a word that recalled the deep contraction of 1929 to 1932. Neither recession nor depression is a word with a precise meaning in an economic sense, in spite of their widespread usage.

vices.) The size of the government sector is larger, and government employment is relatively stable during the cycle. Better methods of inventory control also have contributed to this reduced severity.

A variant of the typical business cycle in the postwar period has been labeled by some economists a *growth recession*, a period of sluggish growth not marked by a downturn in overall economic activity. Such periods occurred in 1965 to 1967 and again in 1984 to 1985. If in 1989 to 1990 the so-called soft landing that was the objective of the Federal Reserve in tightening monetary policy had been successful, there would have been a growth recession.

Cyclical movements should be distinguished from three other types of movements, which can be segregated in the reports of economic data by statistical techniques:

Long-term growth trends;

Seasonal fluctuations, or variations within a year due to weather or other seasonal factors, for example, Easter may fall at different times in different months, making the usual seasonal adjustments inadequate for the surge in spending that occurs before Easter;

Irregular or *random movements,* such as strikes or natural disasters (e.g., hurricanes or earthquakes).

Features of Cyclical Behavior

The most extensive studies of U.S. cyclical history have been conducted under the auspices of the National Bureau of Economic Research, a respected private research organization. These studies have indicated certain repetitive characteristics of business cycles:

1. Most industries and sectors of the economy are affected by business cycles (agriculture and the extraction of natural resources are exceptions);

2. Durable producer and consumer goods are affected more than nondurables and services;

3. Private investment expenditures have greater percentage fluctuations in a cycle than consumer spending;

4. Production fluctuates more than sales, causing still greater movement in inventories;

5. Profits have cyclical movements that conform to business cycles, but profit fluctuations are much greater than those of wages and salaries, dividends, interest payments, and rental income;

6. Industrial prices fluctuate more than retail prices (before World War II, business contractions were periods of price *declines;* in postwar contractions, the rate of price increases has slowed);

7. Short-term interest rates have relatively large movements that conform to cyclical changes. Turning points in long-term interest rates lag behind short-rate turns and have smaller amplitudes; as a result, near cyclical peaks, short rates tend to exceed long rates, resulting in an inverted yield curve.

In addition to economic movements that conform to cycles, certain *timing sequences* with respect to cyclical peaks and troughs have been observed:

1. Months before a cyclical peak, certain activities start to decline, for example, new business formations, com-

mercial and industrial construction contracts, new orders for machinery and equipment;

2. Profit margins decline before profits, which, together
   with stock prices, tend to lead cyclical downturns;

3. Business inventory changes conform positively to cycles and are highly sensitive and volatile, although
   better methods of inventory control have diminished
   the volatility of the inventory cycle. Inventory investment is an important part of short and mild cycles,
   while fluctuations in fixed investment cause longer
   and larger cycles;

4. Monetary aggregates show low cyclical conformity
   and more random fluctuations, limiting their usefulness as a forecasting and possibly as a policy tool.

Causes of Business Cycles

Prior to the 1929 to 1932 severe contraction, little attention
was paid to business cycles, which were believed to be short,
mild and essentially self-correcting. The severity of that contraction initiated many studies of the cycle. Although no one
theory of the causes of business cycles has of yet been generally
accepted, several explanations have been offered by economists.

The explanation usually advanced as to the causes of a
cyclical downturn can be summarized briefly. A long and complex chain of production exists for both long- and short-lived
goods. This chain also produces a stream of income that sup-
ports the demand for the output produced. However, an inter-
ruption in final demand for whatever reason will reduce income, reduce demand further, and lead to curtailed production
and an economic contraction. (Some reasons for a temporary
reduction in demand might be consumers having a plentiful

stock of durable goods such as automobiles, or business having excessive inventories or plant capacity.) Moreover, wages and prices are sticky. They do not respond quickly to changes in the supply or demand for goods and services, and may not adjust enough to avoid excessive unemployment. A down cycle results, which will correct after the excesses in the system are worked off.

The cycle, although temporary, can be harmful to the country's welfare, so that government action is desirable to temper these adverse effects. Monetary action by the Federal Reserve can influence the supply of money and credit and the level of interest rates. Fiscal policy includes the influence on the private sector of federal spending, receipts, and the budget surplus or deficit. Either or both of these policy tools have been used to offset the effects of either a contraction or an overheated expansion.[3]

Other explanations of the cycle disagree with the desirability of government action to offset cyclical changes. The monetarists argue that changes in the money supply are the causes of cyclical fluctuations; thus, a steady rate of growth in the money supply and no monetary policy shifts are the way to dampen cyclical fluctuations considerably.

In the 1970s, another view of the cycle argued that changes in the money supply could affect real variables such as employment. However, public expectations about changes in the money supply are formed rationally and the changes would

[3]Note that this explanation of the down cycle depends on demand shifts due to excessive stocks of goods, plant, and inventories that must be worked off. Some economists have suggested that contractions in demand can be intensified by vulnerability in financial positions, that is, debt-burdened consumers and highly leveraged businesses. Fiscal policy stimulation can be immobilized by efforts to reduce the federal deficit, and changes in the financial structure may limit the effectiveness of monetary policy; thus, these changes could intensify the severity of future contractions.

always be anticipated. Therefore, controlling the money supply does not affect real variables such as employment and output and is therefore undesirable.

In the 1980s, another school of thought argued that changes in the economy are more permanent than temporary and are due to things such as technological change or shocks (e.g., wars or changes in the price of oil). This group doesn't believe in temporary cycles—it questions the desirability of any government intervention to affect employment and output.

These very brief summaries hardly do justice to the vast literature on the causes and control of business cycles. They are presented to illustrate the differences in current thinking on the causes of cycles and the appropriate government response to cyclical fluctuations. In spite of these alternative views, government action, through fiscal and monetary policy changes, to offset cyclical fluctuations are still a cherished belief of most economists, politicians, and private citizens.

At this time, use of fiscal policy to counter the cyclical downturn that apparently started in the summer of 1990 is limited because of the enormous size of the federal deficit and the efforts to reduce it. Therefore, Federal Reserve monetary policy is the primary countercyclical force available. Yet monetary policy is also constrained by concern over inflation, the position of the dollar in foreign exchange, and by the limited tools (mostly working on short-term interest rates) at the Federal Reserve's disposal.

Tracking the Cycle

Considerable research has been devoted to developing tools to analyze business cycles. The National Bureau of Economic Research (NBER) has tracked economic time series for many years, that is, monthly or quarterly data on particular economic activities such as production, inventories, stock prices, and so on. These series often have turning points followed by irregular but extended periods of advances and declines. When turning points of many of these series cluster together at a particular month or quarter, these months or quarters have been labeled reference dates, that is, the date in which general business activity peaked or bottomed out.

The NBER has formed a committee of economists that establish these reference dates, and these dates are generally accepted. Unfortunately, the committee's decisions are made well after turning points have occurred. In April 1991 the committee decided that the peak of the most recent cycle was July 1990.

After the reference dates for peaks and troughs of economic activity were established, further research revealed that some of the economic time series have peaks and troughs of their own that occurred consistently before, coincident with or after the peak or trough reference dates; other series could not be so classified. Those with the most consistent patterns were combined into indexes of leading, coincident, and lagging indicators; these indicators have been revised several times as the economy has changed. The indicators are released monthly by the Department of Commerce and are reported in the financial press. They include measures of employment; production and income; consumption; trade orders and inventories; capital investment; prices, costs, and profits; and money and credit. A weighting system has been adopted to prevent the more volatile series from dominating the indexes. The system is also designed to give the better performing series a heavier weight.

The components of the leading index are as follows:

1. Average weekly hours in manufacturing;

2. Average weekly initial claims for unemployment insurance (series is inverted for analysis, i.e., when claims go down the economy is going up);

3. New orders, consumer goods, and material (expressed in 1982 dollars);

4. Vendor performance, slower deliveries;

5. Contracts and orders for plant and equipment (expressed in 1982 dollars);

6. Building permits, new private housing units;

7. Change in unfilled orders, durable goods (smoothed, expressed in 1982 dollars);

8. Change in sensitive material prices (smoothed);

9. Stock prices, 500 stocks;

10. Money supply, M2 (expressed in 1982 dollars);

11. Index of consumer expectations.

The components of the coincident index are as follows:

1. Employees on nonagricultural payrolls;

2. Personal income less transfer payments (expressed in 1982 dollars);

3. Industrial production;

4. Manufacturing and trade sales (expressed in 1982 dollars).

The components of the lagging index are as follows:

1. Average duration of unemployment (series is inverted for analysis);

2. Ratio, manufacturing, and trade inventories to sales (expressed in 1982 dollars)

3. Change in labor cost per unit of output, manufacturing, (smoothed);

4. Average prime rate;

5. Commercial and industrial loans (expressed in 1982 dollars);

6. Ratio of consumer installment credit to personal income;

7. Change in CPI for services (smoothed).

These indicators have provided a useful method of tracking the cyclical path of the economy. However, some myths have crept into the analysis of the indicators; for example, it is popular to say that three months of a decline in the leading indicators forecast a "recession" in the near future. But because some of the data in the time series used are often revised, it takes a number of months to be sure that three months of actual decline have occurred. Moreover, three months of decline historically have predicted more erroneous turns at peaks and troughs than they have true turns. Using a greater number of months of declines and increases improves the accuracy, but by then the economy is either *in* a downturn or upturn! Remember also that all of the components of the indexes have been released prior to the release of the indexes; following them on an individual basis can provide a good clue to future indicator movements that will be reported.

The measures have also been criticized because they do not actually reflect the complex economy we have. For example, the majority of employment in recent years has been in the services sector, which has been growing in importance, but services activity is not well represented in the indexes. In addition, the United States is becoming more and more a part of a global economy, while the indexes reflect primarily domestic activity. Future revisions of the indexes may address these weaknesses.

Although cycles share some common characteristics, each cycle is individual in nature. Its causes may differ, its duration will differ from the average, its severity will vary, and its turning points will not be recognized until after the fact. Relying on averages of historical relationships may not always be helpful for forecasting the future; it was of little help in assessing the length of the 1982 to 1990 expansion, which was the second longest in history. The weakness in the financial sector in 1990 as well as the high level of debt of business, consumers, and the government may affect the severity of a downturn. The indicators can be more useful for tracking the economy than for predictive purposes.

One method of following the indicators is to watch the monthly reports in the *Survey of Current Business,* published by the Department of Commerce. A special insert of this publication called "Business-Cycle Indicators" provides the last fourteen months of numerical data for all the indicators and their components, as well as for a large number of other important economic time series. In addition, 18 pages of charts have plotted the indicators and their components from 1953 to date and other economic time series monthly or quarterly from 1964 to date. This information provides an extraordinarily useful method of following not just the indicators but other economic data as well.

As an example, Figure 9.5 is a copy of the first page of charts showing the movement of the three composite indexes. The peaks and troughs of the business cycles from 1957 to 1958 are indicated, so that the indicators can be seen relative to business-cycle turning points. In addition, at the bottom of the figure, a separate computation of the ratio of coincident to lagging indexes is plotted; this ratio, at times, had a better predictive record than the leading index.

Figure 9.5. Cyclical Indicators

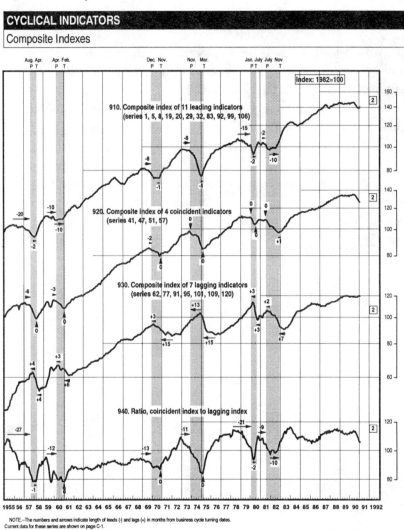

NOTE.—The numbers and arrows indicate length of leads (-) and lags (+) in months from business cycle turning dates.
Current data for these series are shown on page C-1.

Source: SCB, March 1991, p. C-7.

203

SUMMARY

This chapter covered three major characteristics of the economy: long-term trends, price movements and prospects, and cyclical fluctuations. Trends estimated by two government organizations place the growth of real GNP between 2 and 3 percent for the next 6 years; price inflation is expected to be between 4 and 6 percent. Cyclical fluctuations have some common characteristics but each cycle is different. The causes are still debated, but a good way to follow cyclical trends is to watch the economic indicators and their components. The peak of the most recent cycle was probably in July 1990, with the trough not yet determinable at this writing.

CHAPTER 10

Understanding Corporate Profits

In a profit-oriented economy like that of the United States, tracking profits helps answer the question of how well the economy is doing. As discussed in Chapter 1, the economy affects corporate profits, which in turn affect stock prices. Profits are a good indicator of future business investment (as discussed in Chapter 5) because profits are a volatile part of corporate cash flow. Investors track the movements of profits to evaluate stock market changes. Investors also follow the past and expected changes in individual company earnings and dividends to compare them against movements in profits and dividends as a whole. Understanding how profits are measured and examining the factors that influence profit changes can be very useful in appraising the economy and the shifts in the stock market.

This chapter will discuss:

Different measures of corporate profits defined are:

Shareholder reported profits

NIPA profits

Profits reported for tax purposes

Uses of shareholder profits measures

Uses of NIPA profits measures:

NIPA operating profits, profits before tax, profits after tax

Rest of world profits

Financial corporate profits

Nonfinancial profit details

Corporate profits can be measured in three ways: profits reported to shareholders, profits as reported in the National Income and Product Accounts (NIPA), and profits reported for income-tax purposes.

Compilations of *reported profits to shareholder* as well as profits for individual companies and groups of companies are useful for investment purposes. As discussed in Chapter 1, future profits and dividends are one of the causes of changes in stock prices. Profit compilations can be related to appropriate stock market price indexes for an evaluation of the current level and future prospects for stock prices generally or for specific groups of stocks.

NIPA profit measures reflect profits from current production, defined as profits:

Before taxes;

After adjustment to place inventories on a current cost basis rather than the many ways corporations treat inventories on their books; and

After adjustment to place depreciation on a current replacement cost basis and estimates of the useful service lives of plant and equipment.

The resulting profits, called *operating* or *economic profits,* permit uniform comparisons of profits over time.

Major divisions of profits are for *domestic nonfinancial corporations, domestic financial corporations* and *rest of the world* profits; this latter category includes the contribution to profits of overseas earnings after deducting U.S. earnings sent overseas.

For those interested in a detailed analysis of nonfinancial profits the labor costs, capital consumption, net interest, indirect business taxes, and profits are reported per unit of real nonfinancial output. This information provides valuable insights into costs and profit margins that are not available in corporate shareholder reports.

Compilations of profits reported for tax purposes are of limited use for current business analysis because of the long delay before they are available. Individual tax returns are, of course, confidential.

DIFFERENT MEASURES OF CORPORATE PROFITS

Profits are measured in several ways, and it is important to understand the differences among them for economic and investment analysis.

Shareholder Profits

A profits measure most familiar to most people is *profits reported to shareholders,* which reflect how the management of a particular corporation evaluates the company's operations, ordinarily checked by an independent audit as performed by a recognized accounting firm. Generally accepted accounting principles, as defined by the Financial Accounting Standards Board, do bring a certain uniformity to shareholder-reported profits. However, corporations have some degree of flexibility in the degree of consolidation of subsidiaries and the treatment of depreciation.

Shareholder reports are often based on worldwide consolidation of earnings, while tax returns submitted to the IRS are not. In addition, shareholder reports usually reflect straight-line depreciation, that is, depreciation of an asset in equal amounts each year over its estimated useful life. However, tax returns may use any of several depreciation methods to permit accelerated write-offs. (Depreciation is a before-tax charge to earnings that of itself does not represent a cash outlay; therefore, higher depreciation charges reduce taxable earnings but increase the cash flow a company may retain.) Accelerated write-offs may result in lower depreciation for shareholder reports than is reported on tax returns. As a result, higher earnings are reported to shareholders than to the IRS; both procedures are permitted and are perfectly legal.

National Income Account Profits

A second and less well-known measure of profits is reported by the Department of Commerce and included in the information on the quarterly GNP.

Chapter 2 mentioned one way of viewing GNP—to consider it the sum of incomes generated in producing the nation's output; this income equals the costs of production plus profits. Profits include corporate profits, incomes of proprietorships and partnerships, and rental income received by persons. The corporate profits figure is *not* the sum of all of the profits reported by all the corporations in the country. The figure is rather an attempt to measure the *earnings of corporations arising from current production that is distributed to the residents of the United States.*

The basic source of the information about corporate profits is corporate income-tax returns. However, because of the delay in obtaining this information, the most recent year's estimates are an approximation of what these returns will be when they are finally compiled.[1]

In order to reflect profits from current production, two major adjustments are made to the profits figures:

> *Inventories used in production* are not valued by the various methods corporations use to carry inventories on their books (that is, first-in, first-out (FIFO) or last-in, first-out (LIFO)). Instead, inventories are valued at an estimate of the physical volume of inventories adjusted to prices in the calendar year or quarter being reported, referred to as the "current period." The purpose of this adjustment is to eliminate from profit compilations any profits (or losses)

[1]Certain adjustments are made to the tax-based profits in order to conform to national income account concepts. The basic profits figure to which these adjustments are made includes the income of corporations organized for profit as well as those of mutual financial institutions (e.g., mutual insurance companies). Intercorporate dividends are excluded to avoid double counting. Net inflows of dividends from abroad (to corporations as well as individuals) and reinvested earnings of foreign affiliates of U.S. corporations are both included.

due to using inventories in current production that are valued at costs different from current costs.

Depreciation charges are adjusted to place them on a current replacement cost basis. This adjustment is called the *capital consumption adjustment.* The purpose of this adjustment is to prevent overstatement (or understatement) of profits because of insufficient (or excessive) depreciation of plant and equipment. Insufficient depreciation results if the replacement cost of plant and equipment is greater than the original cost. Excessive depreciation may result if accelerated depreciation is permitted for income-tax purposes, so that plant and equipment may be written off before the end of its useful life. Congress has authorized this process from time to time as an incentive for increased capital spending.

It should not be surprising that compilations of shareholder and tax-based reports differ considerably. *Nevertheless, shareholder-reported profits are the basis of earnings per share numbers reported by companies and estimated by financial analysts, and are the profits reflected in stock prices.*[2] Shareholder profits are also the basis of profit compilations made by investment organizations and the business press, such as the *Wall Street Journal* or *Business Week.*

Profits Reported for Tax Purposes

The most comprehensive compilation of profits available is that based on corporate income-tax returns. These reports have a considerable degree of uniformity because they are

[2]However, financial analysts and other investors often make their own adjustments to earnings to increase comparability over time and among companies.

prepared in accordance with the provisions of the Internal Revenue Code.[3]

The information about corporate tax returns is released by the IRS in an annual report called *Statistics of Income—Corporate Income Tax Returns.* Unfortunately, this report is not available until several years after the end of the tax year. For example, data for taxable years that end between July 1990 to June 1991 will not be published until mid-1993. Consequently, the information is of historical interest but of limited use for current business analysis.

USES FOR SHAREHOLDER EARNINGS

With this selection of reports available, which is the best one to look at when evaluating profits trends? For the investor, probably the most useful compilation of profits is the estimate of earnings on the well-known stock market averages, such as the Standard & Poor's and the Dow-Jones Industrial Average. The historical data are available from either of the two organizations that compile the averages or can be found in the reference section of many public libraries and brokerage firms.

Many brokerage firms also report their own estimates of current as well as next year's earnings for individual companies and for composites of earnings. Consequently, the trends of both earnings and price to earnings (P/E) ratios can be reviewed and current earnings and P/E multiples may be compared with

---

[3]The Internal Revenue Code (the code) does permit varying treatment for such items as depreciation, depletion, installment sales, and gains and losses on property sales. Treatment of foreign profits and the degree of consolidation used in reporting for related corporations also affect the comparability of the data. As a generalization, intercorporate dividends and capital gains and losses are included, special revenues are excluded, and foreign subsidiary earnings are included only to the extent that dividends are remitted to the parent company.

the historical record. These aggregates also provide a base against which to compare earnings reports for individual companies.

One caution is necessary when using these estimates of current earnings. Experience over many years indicates that estimates for a particular year, either for an individual company or for an aggregate of companies, are almost invariably optimistic. Rarely is a forecast made for a contraction in business activity or profits, and early estimates (the estimating season usually starts about August for the following year) also do not anticipate unforeseen events. Consequently, these earnings estimates should be taken with a grain of salt until at least one or two quarter's of earnings in a forecast year have actually been published and analyzed.

One further caution should be observed. Traditionally, earnings are reported compared with earnings of the previous year or the same quarter of the previous year; by now readers should be aware of the need for comparisons for a period longer than one year. Moreover, quarterly comparisons can be misleading; earnings may have declined for two quarters but still be above those of the same quarter of the prior year. Unfortunately, quarterly earnings at seasonally adjusted annual rates are found only in the aggregate profits reports in the NIPA.

USES FOR NIPA PROFITS

The monthly estimates of quarterly profits in the NIPA of the Department of Commerce are probably the most useful to gain greater insights into the factors influencing total earnings. The quarterly profits are estimated on a seasonally adjusted annual rate basis, thus avoiding the year-over-year comparison. Total corporate profits are estimated; they are also reported for financial and nonfinancial corporations as well as for major industry groupings.

These profits are before income taxes and are adjusted for inventory valuation and depreciation, as discussed earlier. The resulting profits are often called *operating profits* or *economic profits* or *profits from current production*. Over time, operating profits have had the closest relationship to broad stock price movements, because they reflect underlying economic factors that affect profits and eliminate the distortions due to inventory profits, different depreciation methods, and varying tax rates.

In addition, the Commerce Department also reports profits without adjustments for various inventory valuation and depreciation methods. The result, called *profits before taxes*, indicates what profits would be before taxes if tax-allowed depreciation were used and inventories were valued as companies value them on their income-tax returns. When the estimated sum of all federal, state, and local income taxes on corporate earnings is subtracted from profits before taxes, the remainder is an estimate of *profits after taxes* in the economy. Commerce also reports total *corporate dividends*, which reflect dividend payments by corporations located in the United States and abroad to stockholders who are U.S. residents. The payments are net of dividends received by U.S. corporations.

Figure 10.1 shows these three profit measures annually from 1950 to 1990. The differences between operating profits and pretax profits were minor before 1972, but thereafter the differences were significant. The effects of inflation as well as changes in the tax laws accounted for these differences. The changing differences between pretax and after-tax profits is caused by changing tax rates.

Figure 10.2 provide a better understanding of the causes of the major adjustments between operating profits and pretax profits. The solid line indicates the capital consumption adjustment from 1950 through 1990; the dotted line reflects the inven-

Figure 10.1.   NIPA Corporate Profits

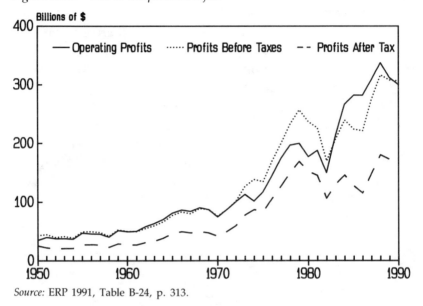

Source: ERP 1991, Table B-24, p. 313.

tory valuation adjustment. Although neither adjustment was very significant before 1962, the rising inflation thereafter, especially that caused by the surges in oil prices in the 1970s, created significant inventory profits that overstated pretax profits. The deflation associated with the 1980 to 1982 business contractions gradually reversed inventory profits, but more recently such profits have increased again.

From 1950 to 1974, depreciation allowances were roughly equal to replacement costs, and the capital consumption adjustment was minor. However, a combination of high inflation in the 1970s and restrictions on allowable depreciation resulted in tax-permitted depreciation less than replacement costs. Inadequate depreciation inflated earnings, and operating profits fell below pretax profits. In the early 1980s slowing inflation and a new depreciation law caused tax depreciation allowances to increase sharply, and the capital consumption adjustment turned positive; operating profits were again greater than pre-

Figure 10.2.   Capital Consumption Adjustment and Inventory Valuation Adjustment

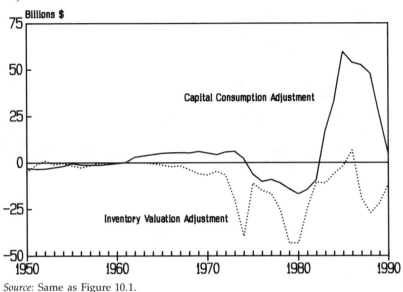

Source: Same as Figure 10.1.

tax profits. In 1986 the depreciation law was changed once again, permitting faster depreciation, but as the effect of this law diminished, the adjustment has fallen again.

The combination of these two adjustments explains the differences between operating and pretax profits after 1971. In effect, pretax profits were overstated from 1973 to 1983, understated from 1984 to 1988 and have been roughly the same in 1989 to 1990. Because of the frequent distortions introduced by inflation and changing depreciation laws, operating profits are a better measure of underlying corporate profitability.

SOURCES OF NIPA PROFITS

Profits as reported in the NIPA come from three sources: nonfinancial corporations, financial corporations, and the rest of the world component. Table 10.1 illustrates how these vari-

Table 10.1.
Corporate Profit Components—1990 (Billions of Dollars)

Nonfinancial Operating Profits	$221.5
Financial Operating Profits	21.6
Total Domestic Operating Profits	243.1
Nonfinancial Inventory Valuation Adjustment	−11.4
Nonfinancial Capital Consumption Adjustment	1.8
Financial Capital Consumption Adjustment	3.1
Total Nonfinancial and Financial Adjustments	−6.5
Nonfinancial Pretax Profits	231.0
Financial Pretax Profits	18.5
Total Domestic Pretax Profits	249.5
Nonfinancial After Tax Domestic Profits	134.1
Financial After Tax Domestic Profits	−17.6
Rest of World Profits	56.9
Total Corporate Profits After Tax	173.4

ous profit components relate to total corporate profits—domestic operating profits, inventory and capital consumption adjustments, domestic pretax profits and total corporate profits after tax.

The rest of the world profits and financial corporate profits are the smaller components of total profits. More extended discussion is required of nonfinancial corporate profits because considerable detail is available to permit a more thorough analysis of the cost factors that influence movements of this profit series.

Rest of World Profits

Rest of world profits reflect receipts by all U.S. residents (corporations and individuals) of:

Earnings (both distributed and reinvested) of foreign affiliates of U.S. direct investors;

Plus the dividend portion of other private receipts;

Less corresponding outflows;

Less income taxes and capital gains and losses.

In short, this component can be viewed like a net import of profits from abroad. It has been growing in importance, as Figure 10.3 indicates. It now equals about $57 billion, about 33 percent of profits after taxes.

Financial Corporate Profits

Financial profits deserve special consideration because, in the NIPA, they are not just a summary of the profits of financial corporations in the United States. Financial pretax profits include two unusual items: profits of the Federal Reserve System

Figure 10.3. Rest of the World Corporate Profits

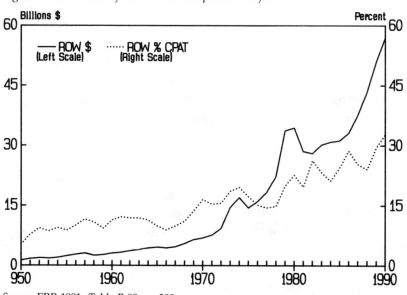

Source: ERP 1991, Table B-89, p. 389.

and the contributions less the payouts of corporate pension plans not insured by insurance companies. Payouts of corporate pension plans are considered like dividend payments; they are included in financial pretax profits because they are corporate income that is not taxed. However, because contributions to these plans now exceed payouts, the net contributions are included in financial pretax profits as a negative number.

Financial profits after taxes have another unusual feature. As we have mentioned earlier, the Federal Reserve pays about 95 percent of its pretax income to the U.S. Treasury. The effective corporate tax rate of the Federal Reserve thus has no relation to the general corporate tax rate.

Consequently, as a result of these two adjustments, the effective corporate tax rate of financial corporations is more than 100 percent. The total financial component of NIPA profits is therefore not especially helpful for tracking movements of either pretax or after-tax financial corporate profits.

ANALYZING NONFINANCIAL PROFITS

The information discussed thus far is sufficient to understand the various profits reports in the press and in financial publications. For those persons interested in major factors impacting profits, the large component of nonfinancial profits can be analyzed in considerable detail. Such detail is not available in company shareholder reports nor in compilations of shareholder profits. However, it is invaluable in understanding cyclical and longer trends in profit performance.

Some of this additional information is available in a quarterly report of the Bureau of Labor Statistics (BLS) *Productivity and Costs*, available from BLS, Washington, D.C. 20212. Each quarter, approximately two months after the end of the quarter, a report is published on nonfinancial output, productivity, labor costs, nonlabor costs, and prices, thus facilitating analysis of unit costs, prices, and unit profits. The Commerce Department, as a part of its quarterly GNP report, adds a breakdown of unit nonlabor costs to that of unit labor costs. Thus, information on costs as well as profits per unit of real output is available. An analysis of this information follows.

Figure 10.4 indicates for each quarter from 1985 to 1990 the change in *nonfinancial corporate physical output* (thin solid line) and the *hours required to product that output* (dashed line). The ratio of the two is *output per hour*, or, as it is often called, *productivity* (thick solid line). The data plotted are shown as year-over-year percent changes, so that each quarterly point plotted indicates the percent change for the prior 12-month period.

Productivity as used here measures the relationship of output in real terms to the labor involved in its production. It does not measure the specific contributions to output attributable to labor, capital, or any other factors of production. In-

Figure 10.4. Output, Hours, and Productivity

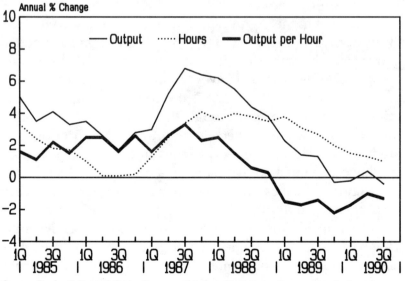

Source: *Productivity and Costs,* Bureau of Labor Statistics releases, quarterly.

stead, productivity reflects the joint efforts of many influences: changes in technology; capital investment; the level of output; utilization of capacity, energy, and materials; the organization of production; managerial skills; and the characteristics and efforts of the work force.

Rising productivity indicates less time involved per unit of output, a favorable sign of efficient use of resources in the economy. Gains in productivity reduce costs and can lead to both lower prices as well as higher real wages.

Changes in productivity are also a leading indicator of cyclical changes in the economy. Increases in productivity slow or even turn into declines as the economy approaches a cyclical peak and then moves into recession. Near a cyclical peak, slower productivity increases are due to the use of less efficient labor and equipment. As economic activity peaks and then declines, productivity usually falls as business is slow to cut costs and reduce employment. However, productivity usually resumes an upward path as the economy begins to expand again, because business does not quickly hire more workers and increase overhead.

Examining the figure, productivity changes were relatively steady from 1985 through 1987. Output changes trended downward through the third quarter of 1986, but hourly changes also decreased. However, following the peak in output in the third quarter of 1987, the picture changed. Output gains decreased sharply through the end of 1989 but hourly changes did not start to decline until the first quarter of 1989. Productivity changes turned negative in the first quarter 1989 and have remained so ever since.

Figure 10.5 takes the analysis one step further. Changes in *productivity*, or output per hour, in this figure are indicated by the thin dotted line. Changes in *compensation per hour* are shown by the thin solid line. Compensation includes monetary remuneration plus supplements such as contributions of the employer to social insurance, pensions, health and welfare

Figure 10.5. Factors Affecting Labor Costs

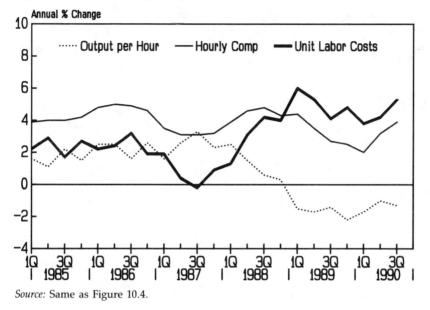

Source: Same as Figure 10.4.

funds, and compensation for injuries. Combining changes in productivity and compensation equals changes in *unit labor costs*, or the cost to produce one unit of output. The rate of increase in unit labor costs rose rapidly from the third quarter of 1987 to the first quarter of 1989 and has remained high ever since.

An additional cost factor is show on Figure 10.6. Changes in unit labor costs are indicated by the solid line; changes in unit nonlabor costs are indicated by the dotted line. Nonlabor costs are defined as follows:

Capital consumption allowances (depreciation and accidental damage to fixed capital);

Net interest payments (interest paid less interest received);

Indirect business taxes (sales, excise and property taxes);

Figure 10.6.   Unit Labor and Nonlabor Costs

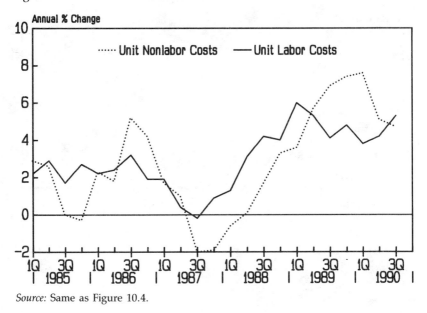

Source: Same as Figure 10.4.

Business transfer payments, primarily gifts to nonprofit organizations and consumer bad debts.

The rise in unit nonlabor costs was even more dramatic than for unit labor costs from 1987 to the first quarter of 1990. One of the reasons for this increase was the dramatic increase in interest costs of nonfinancial corporations, considered in more detail below. In any event, Figure 10.6 indicates that these costs have been rising at annual rates between 4 and 7 percent in 1989 and 1990. Have corporations been able to offset these rising costs?

The answer is shown on Figure 10.7, which plots changes in total (labor and nonlabor) costs as well as prices in the nonfinancial sector. As the figure indicates, costs have increased at a faster rate than prices since the third quarter of 1988. Profit margins have therefore been under pressure.

In addition to the data from the BLS on nonfinancial cor-

Figure 10.7. Total Unit Costs and Prices

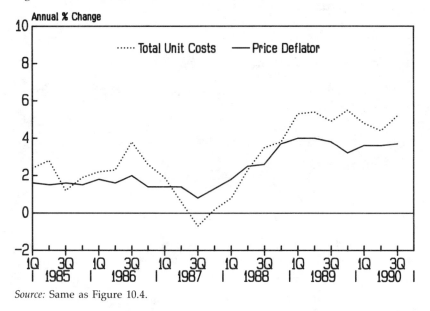

Source: Same as Figure 10.4.

porate productivity summarized in the prior figures, the Commerce Department, as a part of the monthly reports on quarterly GNP, provides additional details about costs and profits. The terms used in the analysis are not too familiar and require a bit of explanation, but the rewards are worth the effort to understand the material.

Together with the report for GNP, the Commerce Department reports gross corporate product originating in the nonfinancial sector of the economy (NFGCP). This series represents the contribution of domestic operations of nonfinancial corporations to GNP.

Just as GNP has an income and a product side, so does NFGCP. On the *product* side, NFGCP represents sales of nonfinancial firms to other businesses and consumers, government and foreigners, plus inventory change less purchases from other firms, domestic and foreign. On the *income* side, NFGCP is defined as the sum of:

Capital consumption allowances;

Indirect business taxes less subsidiaries plus business transfer payments;

Compensation of employees;

Net interest;

Corporate profits before taxes and inventory valuation adjustment.

The BLS data described earlier is useful because of the data it provides on the composition of unit labor costs. The Commerce data supplements this information with a more detailed breakdown of unit nonlabor costs.

Commerce provides information on costs and profits in both current and constant (at present, 1982) dollars. The price deflator for NFGCP reflects the cost in a particular quarter or year for a unit of 1982 dollar NFGCP, that is, the costs incurred and the profits earned in producing one 1982 dollar's worth of output in that period. This cost per unit of NFGCP has been divided into its components of unit costs of capital consumption allowances, indirect business taxes, net interest, and employee compensation; the remaining factor is unit profits. Unit profits are not exactly comparable to the pretax margins (pretax dollars divided by sales) used by financial analysts; unit profits, rather, are current dollar operating profits for a particular period divided by output for that period measured in 1982 prices. Thus, this measure indicates profits per unit of real output rather than profits per dollar of current sales.

For 1990, the costs and profits per unit of 1990 NFGCP expressed in 1982 dollars were as follows:

Table 10.2.
Nonfinancial Corporate Unit Costs and Profits—1990

	Unit Cost	Percent
Unit Capital Consumption Allowances	0.137	11.3
Unit Indirect Business Taxes	0.119	9.8
Unit Interest Costs	0.053	4.3
Total Unit Nonlabor Costs	0.309	25.4
Unit Labor Costs	0.817	67.1
Unit Profits	0.091	7.5
Total Unit Costs and Profits*	1.217	100.0

* This figure equals the price deflator for NFGCP in 1990.

One way to utilize this kind of information is to plot the percentage distribution of unit labor and nonlabor costs as well as profits over time. Figure 10.8 plots this information from 1966 through 1990. The year 1966 was selected as a starting point because in that year the percent of unit profits were the

Figure 10.8. *Percentage Distribution Nonfinancial Corporate Costs and Profits*

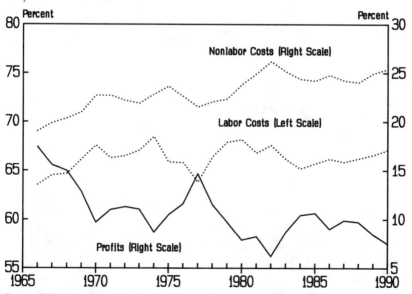

Source: SCB February 1991, Table 7.18, p. 19; earlier data from SCB, July 1982 through July 1990; and BS, Table 7.18.

highest for combined unit costs and profits for any year in the postwar period.

As the figure indicates, the proportion of unit profits in total unit costs and profits has been volatile. This result might be expected, considering that unit profits are a residual caused by changes in both sales volume and costs. The percent of unit profits reached a low point in 1982, increased to 1985 but resumed a downtrend thereafter. In examining the unit cost components, labor costs also moved cyclically but no rising trend is apparent. The rising trend in nonlabor costs caused the downward pressure on unit profits. Of the nonlabor cost components, rising interest payments have had the greatest percentage increase.

Another way to view the effects of rising interest costs on profits is shown in Figure 10.9. The solid line shows nonfinan-

Figure 10.9.   Nonfinancial Profits as a Percentage of GNP

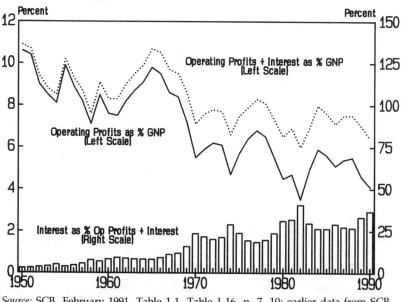

Source: SCB, February 1991, Table 1.1, Table 1.16, p. 7, 10; earlier data from SCB, July 1982 through July 1990 and BS, Tables 1.1, 1.16. Computations by author.

cial profits as a percent of GNP (solid black line), which has had an irregular but pronounced downward trend from 1950 to 1990. If, however, interest charges are added to operating profits, the percent of GNP (dotted line) is more stable since 1970. To indicate the rising importance of interest, interest payments are shown as a percent of operating profits and interest at the bottom of the chart. From a low of 3 percent in 1950, interest costs have climbed to 37 percent of operating profits plus interest in 1990. The debt burden of nonfinancial corporations has clearly increased, and these fixed charges make profits more vulnerable in any economic downturn.

The deterioration of productivity and rising compensation per hour have led to rising unit labor costs. Unit nonlabor costs have also risen. Nonfinancial corporations have not been able to offset these combined increases by higher prices. Economic profits have thus been under pressure recently. Overseas profits and inventory profits have been partial offsets. With a business contraction in progress in late 1990 and early 1991, lower sales volume and inflexible costs should put further pressure on margins and profits. The extent of the deterioration can be measured in future quarterly NIPA reports.

SUMMARY

Profits are a significant measure of economic well-being and an important determinant of stock prices. Profits are measured in several ways. Perhaps the most familiar are profits reported to corporate shareholders; compilations of these profits are prepared by investment organizations and the financial press. Profits are also reported by corporations to the IRS on their tax returns. Compilations of tax profits are prepared and published by the IRS.

NIPA profits contain reports of several profit aggregates that are based on income-tax profits. These profits are profits from current production adjusted to eliminate inventory profits and to reflect replacement cost depreciation. For nonfinancial corporations, costs and profits can be measured per unit of real output, thus providing a measure of corporate costs and profitability. Following these measures quarterly provides an analysis of factors influencing profits and thus indicates future profit trends.

CHAPTER 11

Tracking the Economy

Business news is reported by the media more often than it used to be; however that has its disadvantages as well as its advantages. A 30-second slot on TV news does not provide time for interpretation and analysis, just that the numbers be reported in as dramatic a fashion as possible.

At times, the news reporter believes it necessary to have an economist comment on the numbers. Now one thing the economist is *not* likely to say is that this latest piece of economic information isn't terribly significant and that it adds little to what we already know. The economist usually tries to make the data sound important, with far-reaching implications for the future of the economy.

Reporters have their favorite economic interpreters. If the data are up, the reporter finds an optimist who will endorse the new data as supporting a favorable point of view. If the data are down, a pessimistic economist can be relied upon to provide an appropriate negative conclusion.

The end result is confusion to the listener or reader, and disillusionment about the worth of listening to economic commentators at all. The purpose of this book is to provide some perspective against which the daily bits of economic information can be evaluated. The need for looking at the longer term movements of data—for four or five years at least—has been stressed, and for longer periods for some other data. Another aim of this book was to indicate which economic time series are timely and important in following any particular sector. These tools enable one to evaluate the economic news and have less need for economic commentators and their interpretations.

The purpose of this chapter on tracking the economy is to review once again the important statistics to follow, the sources of data, and some pitfalls to watch in their evaluation.

In previous chapters we have described a number of time series that reflect what is going on in the economy. This chapter summarizes the most useful information, so that it can be found all in one place. Professional economists have commercial services that provide economic data, but the cost is well beyond the means of the average individual. Instead, we will list a few relatively inexpensive sources that the individual can use to develop a personal do-it-yourself economic tool kit. Finally, although warnings about interpreting economic data were scattered throughout the book, the most important ones will be repeated again, all in one place.

STATISTICS TO FOLLOW

Some economic information is more significant that others. Selection is influenced by the purposes for following the economy: business decision, investment decision, personal finances, and so on.

The total economy should be followed for business decisions, as well as changes in the particular segments such as personal consumption expenditures and their components; residential construction expenditures; business spending for plant, equipment and inventories; government spending, and imports and exports. In addition, interest rates are important, as well as information on particular sectors or industries. For investment decisions, the economy, interest rates, and stock prices need to be followed. Interest rates, especially mortgage rates and short-term interest rates, are the most useful to monitor for personal finances.

Many figures and tables in this book are examples of the kinds of information that is useful and also indicate ways that the information can be prepared for review and analysis.

Tracking the Total Economy

The broadest measure used to follow changes in the economy is GNP. The most recent quarterly data are provided each month toward the end of the month. The focus is on the output side, that is, how is GNP removed from the market. Each component should be examined to determine the source of changes. Most of the data in the report have been anticipated by statistical releases covering parts of GNP, but this report puts it all together.

The data are revised each month, with annual revisions covering the previous three years. Major revisions are made less frequently. It is useful to analyze the quarterly and annual revisions, especially if the GNP is used as a framework within which to follow the economy. If economic information is followed, regularly, an overall view of the economy and how it is progressing will be set; at times the revisions will significantly change the concept of what was going on.

Another comprehensive statistic available monthly is the industrial production index, which reports on the physical volume of output in manufacturing, mining, and utility industries. While these industries are not the whole economy, they are vital and cyclically sensitive areas. The index is available at midmonth covering the prior month, and thus is a timely indicator of activity. At the same time, the factory operating rate for the past month also is released.

The leading, coincident, and lagging indexes of activity are combinations of data already released and therefore are not "new" information. They are published about one month after the end of the month they cover. However, like GNP, they put together important historical information with appropriate weightings, and thus provide useful clues to interpreting the cyclical position of the economy.

The major limitation of these indexes is that no two business cycles are alike. The analytical value of comparing current data with averages of past performance is not especially worthwhile. Moreover, some important areas of the economy are not covered by the indicators. Consequently, they are useful but not vital tools of economic analysis.

Tracking Prices

The best measures of current prices movements are the CPI and the producer price index for finished goods, which anticipates changes in the goods components of the CPI by a few months. Examine price movements with and without food and energy components; the latter gives some idea of the underlying or "core" inflation rate. Producer prices of intermediate products and crude materials often foreshadow later movements in finished goods prices. The GNP fixed-weight price index is the broadest measure of prices in the economy. However, it is available only quarterly and is often revised, while the CPI and PPI indexes are changed much less frequently.

Tracking the Consumer

One of the most closely followed economic series is the monthly employment report, which comes out early in the month for the previous month. While most attention is paid to the unemployment rate, the most significant part of the employment report is the information about the changes in jobs on nonagricultural payrolls. Because the data for the two previous months are revised each month, revisions should be examined in interpreting the current report. For example, if prior reports are consistently revised downward, this information is as important as a current decline.

Another early indicator of consumer activity is the thrice-monthly report of domestic automobile sales, which are provided on a seasonally adjusted annual rate basis by the Commerce Department. These reports are both early and not revised, so that they provide a good clue to consumer spending, especially for durable goods. Another series that should be watched carefully is the monthly series on housing starts and building permits, important indicators of consumer commitments for large expenditures.

The Conference Board index of consumer confidence is also a useful indicator of consumer attitudes and expectations. It is of considerable value in anticipating future spending patterns.

Other reports cover the consumer area but are of less value than those cited. Retail sales are very volatile and often revised significantly. Personal income and consumption reports come out at the end of the month and contain few surprises, given other data reported earlier in the month. The consumer credit report is also released late and is more confirmatory than informative.

Tracking the Business Sector

An early and very helpful clue when following the manufacturing sector is the monthly purchasing agents' survey. The strength or weakness of production, new orders, deliveries, inventories, employment, and prices is indicated. The index of these components also has a good relationship to anticipating cyclical changes in business generally.

Changes in manufacturing activity can be followed by the monthly reports of manufacturers' new orders, sales, inventories, and backlogs. Durable goods new orders are good cyclical indicators; new orders indicate future sales. Backlog changes reflect demand pressures. Inventories and inventory-to-sales ratios indicate possible cyclical pressures in the economy. Business sales and inventories are reported about six weeks late and are subject to revisions, so that the earlier data on the manufacturing sector are more useful.

Business fixed investment can be anticipated by following monthly nondefense capital goods new orders, shipments, inventories, and backlogs as well as monthly capacity utilization reports. Surveys of business spending plans are made quarterly but have become less reliable indicators, especially for quarterly spending, as data reliability has become a problem.

Tracking the International Sector

The monthly trade report, looking at export and import trends separately, is the most current information on this sector. More complete information on the balance of payments is available only quarterly with a three-month lag. Following the dollar can be done on a daily basis; quotations against most major currencies are found in the financial section of most newspapers.

Tracking the Financial Markets

When tracking the financial markets, the problem is not absence of data but rather selecting from the abundance available. The best way to follow monetary policy is to obtain some report that will summarize both key interest rates, as well as indications of monetary policy such as the money supply and the federal funds rate. Reading the statements and testimony of members of the Federal Reserve Board is also helpful. The financial press usually carries a weekly statement of data provided by the Federal Reserve, including the money supply measures, member bank reserve changes, and reserve aggregates. For the stock market, movements of stock prices measured by various market indexes are published in the financial press as well as in many brokerage reports. Again the problem is one of selection. The various stock market indexes will be discussed in Chapter 12.

Table 11.1 summarizes the approximate availability of the various economic releases.

SOURCES OF INFORMATION

One of the problems facing anyone interested in following the economy and the markets is where to obtain the necessary information. As a partial answer, the Reference section of this volume lists some primary sources and where information is readily accessible in order to prepare each of the figures and tables in the chapters of this book. For the do-it-yourselfer, suggested basic sources of information are as follows:

The Wall Street Journal or the financial section of major city

Table 11.1.
Monthly Release Times of Economic Statistics

Early in the Month
Employment report for prior month
Purchasing Managers Survey for prior month
Automobile sales for last third of prior month
Construction expenditures for two months earlier
Factory orders and shipments for two months prior
Middle of Month
Industrial production and factory operating rate for prior month
Producer price indexes for prior month
Automobile sales for first third of current month
Consumer confidence index for prior month
Retail sales for prior month
Manufacturing and trade inventories and sales for two months
  prior
Housing starts and building permits for the prior month
Trade balance for two months prior
Late In the Month
Consumer price index for prior month
GNP and components for prior quarter; profits are released with
  the second and third monthly releases of quarterly GNP data
Durable goods new orders
Automobile sales for second third of the current month
Personal income and personal consumption expenditures for the
  prior month
Leading, coincident, and lagging economic indicators for the prior
  month

---

newspapers. The Journal is probably the most complete reference source for daily economic and financial information. However, the *Journal* only occasionally publishes historical charts, so that other sources must be used to get back data for historical statistical series.

The Survey of Current Business is a monthly publication of the Bureau of Economic Analysis of the U.S. Department of Commerce. Annual subscriptions are available for $23 from the

Superintendent of Documents, U.S. Government Printing Office, Washington, D.C. 20402. Of all the data sources, this one is the most comprehensive and the most useful to anyone wishing to set up a statistical database.

The Survey has several parts:

The first few pages contain a review of the current business situation, with charts and commentary;

A monthly feature is a set of 54 selected tables from the NIPA. Each July the full set of 132 tables is presented, with revisions for the prior 3 years;

Special articles about economic statistics are featured, as well as special sets of tabular information on subjects such as the balance of payments, regional statistics, and historical data revisions;

An insert of about 24 yellow pages provides information on business cycle indicators. This information includes not only the leading, coincident, and lagging indicators but also includes other statistical information on employment and unemployment, production and income, consumption, trade orders and deliveries, fixed-capital investment, inventories, prices, costs and profits, money and credit, and other important areas including a number of international indicators. Data are provided in tabular form for the past 14 months and also in chart form for various longer time periods. The 18-page chart section is especially helpful in providing perspective on most of the important economic time series.

The final section, in 32 blue-colored pages, covers current business statistics, providing historical statistics of general business information as well as individual time series of interest to many industry specialists.

For historical data not covered in the monthly *Survey,* two other Commerce Department publications are valuable:

Business Statistics, 1961–88, provides monthly or quarterly data for 1985–88 and annual data for 1961–88 for series that appear in *The Survey of Current Business.* It also contains definitions of terms, sources of data, and methods of compilation. It is available from the Superintendent of Documents.

The National Income and Product Accounts of the United States 1929–82: Statistical Tables. This book contains detailed estimates of the national income and product accounts for 1929–82 based on the comprehensive revision of the accounts released in 1985. It also includes definitions of the major components of the accounts and of the major sectors of the economy. Available from the Superintendent of Documents. (The next comprehensive revision of the NIPA is scheduled for November 1991.)

Persons interested in obtaining current statistical information from the U.S. Department of Commerce via modem to their computer can subscribe to *The Economic Bulletin Board.* Inquiries should be directed to the Office of Business Analysis, U.S. Department of Commerce, Washington, D.C. 20230. Telephone: (202) 377-3870.

The Economic Report of the President is published in February of each year and is available from the Superintendent of Documents. Although the economic commentary in the report is interesting, the extraordinary value of this report is the statistical appendix. Almost every major economic series is covered, with most annual data going back to the end of World War II and some data back to 1929. Monthly or quarterly data are provided for the most recent two or three years. This book is an invaluable reference for historical economic data that would require hours of searching to get from other sources.

For current financial data, the weekly report called *U.S. Financial Data,* available from the Federal Reserve Bank of St. Louis, P.O. Box 66953, St. Louis, MO, 63166-6953. This pamphlet provides 14 months of weekly reports on interest rates, money supply components, and other banking data.

Economic Indicators is a monthly publication of selected economic data available from the Superintendent of Documents. It provides data and charts on output, income spending, employment data, production and business activity, money, credit and security markets, federal finance, and international statistics. Data for many of the figures described in this book will be found here.

The *Federal Reserve Bulletin* is a monthly report available from Publications Services, Mail Stop 138, Board of Governors of the Federal Reserve System, Washington, D.C. 20551. The statistical appendix has a wide array of financial and business statistics, although the time periods covered are not very long; other sources must be consulted if data are needed for several years.

Additional References

Two additional books provide more extended descriptions of some of the economic material covered in this book:

The U.S. Economy Demystified, Albert T. Sommers, (Lexington, MA: Lexington Books, D.C. Heath and Company, 1988). This book, by the former Chief Economist of the Conference Board in New York, is an excellent exposition of the U.S. economic system and the significance of economic statistics.

Guide to Economic Indicators, Norman Frumkin (Armonk, NY: M.E. Sharpe, Inc., 1990) provides more detailed descriptions of many of the economic time series described in this book as well as other statistical series that may be of interest.

WATCH FOR PITFALLS

Several problems in interpreting particular economic reports have been mentioned throughout this book, but it is well to summarize them again.

Time Span Covered

Unfortunately, reports in the media stress the month-to-month or quarter-to-quarter percentage changes. Such information can be very misleading, especially for very volatile series. At least several months of data should be reviewed; the best procedure for monthly data is to review it over several years.

For more volatile series, interpretation can be helped by using moving averages of the data; an average of the past three or six months of data can reveal an underlying pattern that volatile monthly changes may conceal.

Revisions

One of the most exasperating jobs in following economic data is to keep up with the revisions. When month-to-month changes are reported, it is not often mentioned that the past two or three month's data were revised. Other times, the prior year's or several years' data are revised. Some reports, like those in the *Wall Street Journal,* usually indicate that the data have been revised, but many other reports do not.

Historical comparisons have to be made carefully when a series is revised for recent months as well as for several years. The revisions should be reviewed to see how significant they are. At times, changes can materially alter the pattern of activity of a particular series. Usually the revised data or at least where earlier data can be obtained are available shortly in the sources mentioned above.

When revisions are made in monthly reports, it is a good idea to keep track of whether the revisions have had a consistent pattern. For example, if for several months data are consistently revised downward or upward, it indicates that later information was weaker or stronger than earlier and less complete information. Thus the nature of the revisions can provide clues to the strength or weakness of the economy that one-month's data alone do not provide.

Keep in mind that almost all series will be revised, often more than once. The few that are not revised include automobile sales, interest rates, and stock prices.

Seasonal Adjustments

Almost all economic data are reported on a seasonally adjusted basis. However, at times the seasonal adjustment may not be adequate. A winter milder than average will cause data influenced by the weather, such as housing starts, to appear stronger than they otherwise would.

At times, data are reported on a year-over-year basis, in order to avoid the seasonal problem. However, this introduces a risk of obscuring recent performance. It is possible for a statistic to be well above year-earlier levels but still plunging for several months! Ten-day automobile sales continue to be reported in the press compared with sales in the similar ten days of a year ago, virtually meaningless for analytical purposes.

The warning is obvious: Watch for the types of seasonal adjustment and see whether it might have been influenced by unusual circumstances.

Temporary Factors

At times, information can be distorted by unusual factors. For example, the monthly employment report for most of 1990 was influenced by the hiring and later release of temporary government workers for the decennial census. The government did provide information on the number of census workers on the payroll each month, so that an adjustment could be made in interpreting the changes in employees on payrolls. However, this adjustment was not ordinarily reported in the media, and the unadjusted report was unreliable for a good part of the year.

Other unusual factors can affect data, such as strikes, storms and other weather phenomena, earthquakes, and similar events. Contemporaneously, data interpretation can allow for such developments. However, in reviewing data for a number of past years, it is difficult, if not impossible, to know whether a particular month's data were influenced by such a development. The best advice is to be aware of such a possibility and interpret unusual developments with caution.

Don't Count the Same Thing Twice

When interpreting economic data, it is important not to read each piece of information as "new" information. We have mentioned that changes in the components of GNP have been forshadowed by reports on many of the GNP component areas. Automobile sales heavily influence durable goods retail sales. Building permits reflect future housing starts. Employment changes and average hours worked in manufacturing provide indications of later movements in the industrial production index. Knowledge of these relationships can provide better insights into the economy and prevent unnecessary enthusiasm over something that already has been reported.

SUMMARY

This chapter has reviewed the statistics described in earlier chapters, indicating which ones are the most useful in following the total economy and which ones the best in following particular segments. Sources of information were discussed, recommending a few that provide historical economic data that can be used to interpret current economic reports in the financial press. Some cautions in interpreting economic data were also offered, so that these pitfalls would be avoided in determining the meaning of the latest reports.

CHAPTER 12

Suggestions for the Individual Investor

The earlier chapters in this book were designed to help in understanding how the various sectors of the economy relate to each other and how to view changes in the economy with a long-term perspective. The main requirements needed to track the economy is this sense of perspective, access to the financial press, a few government data sources, and some spare time.

Chapter 1 outlined the relationships between the economy, inflation, interest rates, profits, and stock prices. The present chapter will offer further background information for the individual investor to assist in making better-informed investment decisions. No great exposition of financial analysis or portfolio management is intended—nor can tips be provided on how to pick hot stocks or time the market. We offer just a few ideas to give broader perspective for investing, just as earlier chapters were designed to provider broader perspective on the economy.

Four major topics are covered in this chapter:

Understanding *investment objectives,* a process many investors overlook or believe that they are incompetent to do. However, only investors themselves are best qualified to determine their objectives;

Understanding *risk,* a topic often forgotten when establishing and managing a portfolio.

Understanding the advantages of *portfolio diversification.*

Following the *stock market,* a description of the various stock market averages and their advantages and disadvantages.

UNDERSTANDING INVESTMENT OBJECTIVES

What are *investment objectives?* Investment objectives are a description of the purposes of an investment portfolio and the risks an investor is willing to assume to achieve them. In setting objectives, the investor should do the following:

List specific rather than general objectives;

Determine whether these objectives are to be met now or at some future time;

Set an absolute rate of return for your portfolio that you need in order to meet your objectives, and examine that return to see if it is realistic;

Fix a time horizon over which results are to be measured;

Determine your risk tolerance for the portfolio.

Portfolio Purposes

A portfolio may have one or several objectives. The portfolio may be designed to provide current income for someone, or to build a retirement fund. The purpose may be to build an estate that ultimately will be left to someone or to charity. It may be destined to provide a college education for children, or build a fund to buy a house. A corporate retirement fund is designed to provide present and future retirement benefits for employees.

The purpose should be as specific as possible. Objectives such as making as much money as possible or not losing money are too vague and do not consider risk. It is a good idea to commit these objectives to writing, so that they can be reviewed from time to time to see whether they need changing or whether they are being achieved.

Can The Investor Get There?

Once the purpose or purposes of the portfolio are established, the next step is determining when these objectives are to be reached—now, or at some future time. Then it must be determined, using realistic assumptions about future investment returns, whether the funds available are sufficient to reach the objectives set; if not, the objectives may have to be scaled back.

In matching funds versus objectives, the effects of inflation should be kept in mind. For example, when thinking of a fund to be available in the future or one that provides an income stream over a long period of time, be sure to factor in an estimate of future inflation rates. The principal sum or the income needed in dollars of future purchasing power is then determined.

The statement of investment objectives requires determining an *absolute rate of return* that will be needed on the funds available to reach the desired goal. *Relative rates of return,* such as beating the stock market or getting a better rate of return than that available from some other investment, are useful objectives in a subsidiary sense, but an absolute rate of return is essential. Selecting expected rates of return can be materially helped by reviewing historical rates of return, covered in the next section of this chapter.

LONG-TERM INVESTMENT RETURNS

Investors often find it difficult to establish realistic rate of return objectives, because they have limited information about what rates of return have been achieved on various types of investments in the past. This section provides, in tabular and chart form, rates of return on several financial instruments for most of the years since World War II and for important sub-periods during that time. These rates of return have varied; some explanations for the variations are offered to enable you to estimate expected returns more easily.

The following information covers financial instruments only, that is, stock and bonds. They were selected because these securities are marketable and the records of their prices, as well as interest and dividend payments, are available for long periods of time. Returns for other types of investments are not as readily available.[1]

[1]Returns on real estate equity investment, for example, are available only for shorter periods and cover only limited samples of real estate. Real estate is a unique product that does not have a ready market with frequent transactions; this lack of liquidity results in a

Table 12.1.
Average Annual Return 1950 to 1990

30-Day U.S. Treasury Bills	5.31%
Intermediate (5 year) U.S. Government Bonds	6.13%
Long-Term (20 year) U.S. Government Bonds	5.24%
Long-Term (20 year) Corporate Bonds	5.85%
Common Stocks (S&P 500 Stock Index)	13.39%

Long-Term Average Returns

Table 12.1 indicates the average return on various types of financial instruments for the years 1950 to 1990, which covers practically the entire postwar period. The return was computed by taking the total return (income plus appreciation or less deprecation) for each year and computing a simple arithmetic average of the total of the individual year's returns.

Of course, averages can be misleading; the story of someone drowning in a lake with an average water depth of three feet is well-known. Thus, further information as well as an average is needed.

In addition, the results shown in Table 12.1 may seem a bit odd because the returns on long-term bonds, both government and corporate, averaged less than the returns on intermediate issues and, in the case of long-term government bonds, less than the return on Treasury bills. Ordinarily an investor would expect to receive a higher return to compensate for the longer wait before the principal of the investment is returned at ma-

---

return that should be somewhat higher than the return on common stocks. As a rough rule of thumb, real estate equity returns over time have been between 2 and 3 percentage points higher than the return on common stocks. The returns on other types of investments can be estimated in much the same way—returns in excess of the historic returns on stocks or bonds reflect the greater risk taken in these other types of investment.

turity. In actual practice the opposite has been true. How can this anomaly be explained?

Annual and Average Returns

Figures 12.1 through 12.5 present the annual returns for each of the financial instruments for the 1950 to 1990 period, with the average return indicated by the thin solid line as a first step toward answering this puzzle. These figures also provide some perspective on returns over time. The vertical scales for the figures are approximately the same, so that the volatility or fluctuations around the average of the annual returns of the various financial instruments can be compared. (Volatility risk is discussed at greater length later in this chapter.)

Figure 12.1 presents the investment returns for U.S. Treasury bills. Year-to-year fluctuations in returns are not very

Figure 12.1. Investment Returns—U.S. Treasury Bills

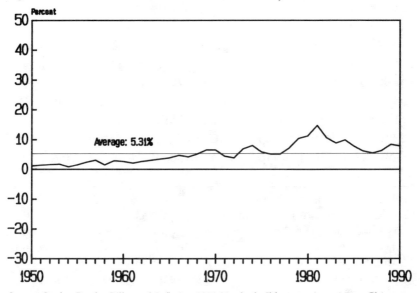

Source: Stocks, Bonds, Bills, and Inflation 1991 Yearbook, Ibbotson Associates, Chicago, IL, pp. 194–207. Computations by author.

great. Returns trended gradually upward until 1981, fell until 1987 but have been higher since. Returns before 1969 were all below the average return, while returns in most years since have been above average.

Figure 12.2 indicates the annual returns and the average return for intermediate government bonds. The year-to-year fluctuations in this series are greater than those for Treasury bills. However, a similar pattern is evident: returns prior to 1970 were generally below average and returns after 1970 were higher than average.

When attention is shifted to the returns of long-term government bonds in Figure 12.3, the most striking characteristic is the greater volatility, particularly in the period after 1969. The very high returns in 1982 and 1984 to 1986 pulled the average return up considerably. Presumably something happened in this later period to cause average returns to be much higher.

Figure 12.2.   Investment Returns—U.S. Intermediate Government Bonds

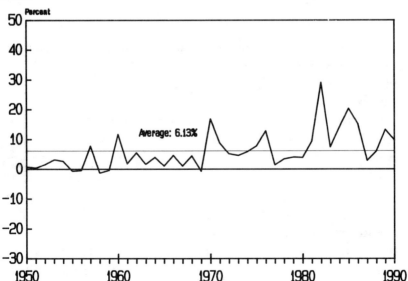

Source: *Stocks, Bonds, Bills, and Inflation 1991 Yearbook,* Ibbotson Associates, Chicago, IL, pp. 194–207. Computations by author.

Figure 12.3.   Investment Returns—U.S. Long-Term Government Bonds

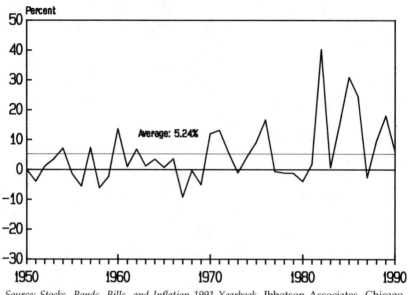

Source: *Stocks, Bonds, Bills, and Inflation 1991 Yearbook,* Ibbotson Associates, Chicago,
IL, pp. 194–207. Computations by author.

A similar observation can be made about long-term corporate bonds as seen in Figure 12.4. Returns were quite volatile,
but after 1982, returns averaged considerably higher than in
prior periods.

Figure 12.5 indicates the returns for common stocks. Here
the volatility is greater than that of any other series, although
common stock volatility diminished after 1980 while the volatility of long-term bonds increased. The average return of
common stocks was more than double the return of any of the
other investments considered. Returns followed a saucer-
shaped pattern—trending downward to 1974 and rising thereafter. Common stocks had fewer years of negative returns than
either of the long-term bonds series—10 negative years out of
41 for stocks and 14 and 13 negative years, respectively, for
government and corporate long-term bonds.

Figure 12.4.   Investment Returns—Long-Term Corporate Bonds

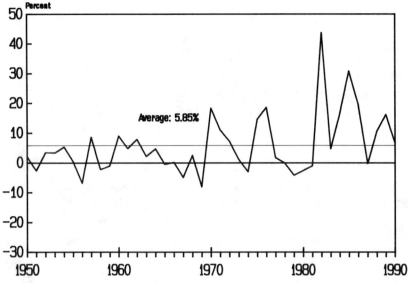

Source: *Stocks, Bonds, Bills, and Inflation 1991 Yearbook*, Ibbotson Associates, Chicago, IL, pp. 194–207. Computations by author.

Figure 12.5.   Investment Returns—Common Stocks

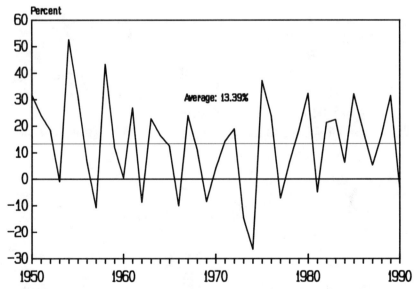

Source: *Stocks, Bonds, Bills, and Inflation 1991 Yearbook*, Ibbotson Associates, Chicago, IL, pp. 194–207. Computations by author.

Volatility and Return

Investments with greater volatility have provided higher returns. Is there some way by which these two factors can be measured and then compared among various investments?

A statistical measure called the *standard deviation* measures the dispersion of individual points (in this case, yearly returns) around the average; the method gives greater weight to wider differences than narrow differences. In order to obtain a measure that compares the dispersion and risk of several series, this dispersion or standard deviation is divided by the average return. The result provides a measure of *volatility per unit of return*. This measure for the financial instruments we have surveyed is shown in Table 12.2

Stocks, which are more volatile that bonds, had a sufficiently larger return so that the risk per unit of return, although greater than Treasury bills and intermediate government bonds, was less than for long-term government and corporate bonds.

The Inflation Rate

The returns discussed previously are called "nominal" returns, that is, they are not adjusted to show the real purchasing power of the dollars of return received. A simple way to illustrate the purchasing power of these returns is to adjust

Table 12.2.
Volatility Per Unit of Return
Selected Financial Instruments 1950 to 1990

U.S. Treasury Bills	0.60
Intermediate U.S. Government Bonds	1.03
Long-Term U.S. Government Bonds	1.91
Long-Term Corporate Bonds	1.72
Common Stocks	1.27

them for inflation by subtracting the annual inflation rate (as measured by the familiar CPI) from the annual returns.

Figure 3.3 in Chapter 3 shows the annual change in the consumer price index from 1950 to 1990. What did these differing inflation rates mean for investment returns? The next few charts show the so-called real returns, or returns less the annual inflation rates.

Figure 12.6 indicates the real return on U.S. Treasury bills for the 1950 to 1990 time period. During the years 1952 to 1972, the bill rate closely followed the inflation rate, running slightly above it for most years. From 1973 to 1980, bill returns did not keep up with inflation. In the period since 1980, returns on bills have averaged almost 4 percentage points above the inflation rate; investors now require higher real returns on even the safest securities, probably because their expectations are for higher inflation rates in the future.

Figure 12.6.   Inflation-Adjusted Investment Returns—U.S. Treasury Bills

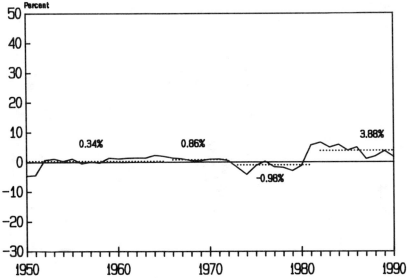

Source: *Stocks, Bonds, Bills, and Inflation 1991 Yearbook*, Ibbotson Associates, Chicago, IL, pp. 194–207. Computations by author.

Figure 12.7 shows the returns for intermediate U.S. government bonds. The pattern is much the same as that of bills, with the fluctuations in returns somewhat greater because of the longer maturity of intermediate bonds. Real returns on average were positive from 1950 through 1972 at a level somewhat higher than bill rates. Real returns fell more than 3 percentage points below the inflation rate for the 1973 to 1981 period. Returns from 1982 to 1990 were well-above the inflation rate, averaging 9.10 percent.

Figure 12.8 shows the same information for long-term government bonds. Here the pattern is both surprising and disappointing; returns averaged below inflation for the entire period up to 1981. A similar pattern is shown for long-term corporate bonds in Figure 12.9, although they did have a return slightly in excess of the inflation rate in 1950 to 1965. Real

Figure 12.7.   Inflation-Adjusted Investment Returns—U.S. Intermediate Investment Bonds

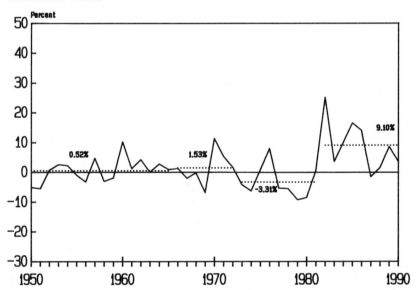

Source: Stocks, Bonds, Bills, and Inflation 1991 Yearbook, Ibbotson Associates, Chicago, IL, pp. 194–207. Computations by author.

Figure 12.8.   Inflation-Adjusted Investment Returns—U.S. Long-Term Government Bonds

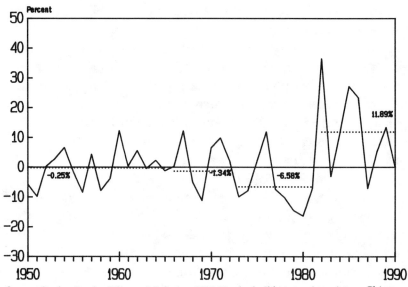

Source: *Stocks, Bonds, Bills, and Inflation 1991 Yearbook*, Ibbotson Associates, Chicago, IL, pp. 194–207. Computations by author.

Figure 12.9.   Inflation-Adjusted Investment Returns—Long-Term Corporate Bonds

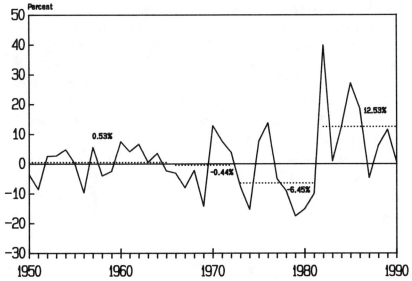

Source: *Stocks, Bonds, Bills, and Inflation 1991 Yearbook*, Ibbotson Associates, Chicago, IL, pp. 194–207. Computations by author.

returns have significantly exceeded those of bills and intermediate bonds only in the period since 1982.

Why has this pattern for long-term securities occurred? In addition to the long-term debilitating effects of inflation, another reason for this pattern was that in the earlier years of this period, long-term investors such as insurance companies and pension funds bought these bonds for their higher yield and planned to keep them to maturity. Therefore, they carried these bonds on their books at cost and paid little attention to fluctuations in market prices.

However, U.S. insurance companies are no longer major purchasers of long-term bonds. Their product mix has shifted from mostly ordinary life policies to other types where the policyholder shares in the investment return that is linked to the current investment return on the company's portfolio. More recent purchasers of long-term bonds trade them rather than hold them to maturity, attempting to make capital gains on the trades. Therefore, they carry the securities at market, and price fluctuations over time are important. In addition, investors have become aware of the need to receive a real return that compensates for the possibility of higher inflation rates in the future. Capital markets also have become international, and U.S. securities must compete for capital with demands worldwide. Consequently higher real returns are necessary to induce investors to purchase longer maturity bonds.

Figure 12.10 indicates the real returns for common stocks. Although very volatile, common stock real returns were negative on average only during 1973 to 1981, and the average negative return in that period was less than those of all but Treasury bills. Thus, for those investors who can stand the volatility of stock returns, they do appear to provide a good hedge against inflation in all but periods of very high inflation rates.

Figure 12.10.   Inflation-Adjusted Insurance Returns—Consumer Stocks

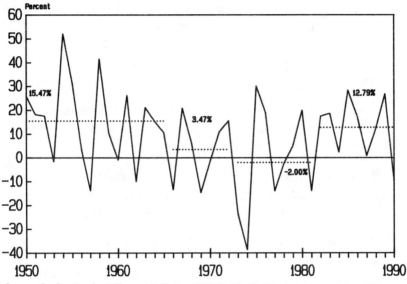

Source: *Stocks, Bonds, Bills, and Inflation 1991 Yearbook*, Ibbotson Associates, Chicago, IL, pp. 194–207. Computations by author.

Selecting a Rate of Return

When selecting a rate of return for a portfolio, the following ideas may be useful:

In setting return expectations, using absolute numbers based on long-term averages may not be the best guide. Returns in the most recent decade may be more meaningful;

The higher the expected return, the greater the volatility of returns;

Investment returns for financial instruments have varied considerably during the past 40 years, and these variations have been related, in part at least, to the inflation rate.

More recently (1982 to 1990), all types of investments have had returns that were greater than the inflation rate by an amount more than in prior years.

To establish an expected absolute rate of return, the following procedure is suggested:

- Check any nominal rate selected against the past record of returns for various financial instruments to determine how realistic the selected rate is;

- Select an expected inflation rate. References to Figure 3.3 and the discussion of the long-term inflation outlook in Chapter 9 may be useful for this purpose;

- Estimate the real rate of return, that is, the return above the inflation rate, implicit in the nominal rate selected;

- Review the figures on inflation-adjusted rates of return to see whether the expectations are reasonable relative to past inflation and returns, especially in recent years.

TIME HORIZON

Part of setting investment objectives is selecting an investment time horizon, that is, the period over which investment results will be measured. Most investors are understandably impatient, which puts them at the mercy of the short-term vagaries of the markets, forgetting that short-term results could be due to chance and could cause a switch in investments just at the wrong time.

A realistic alternative is to select a longer time period to measure results, for example, five years or a complete market cycle. Of course, an investor shouldn't wait for five years before determining whether the investment program is on track; investments must be reviewed regularly to see if results are on the path that will achieve the set objectives.

Figure 12.11 may provide some perspective on investment time horizons. The annual nominal investment returns (income plus price gains or losses) for the stock market for each of the years 1926 through 1990 were reviewed along with the average annual results for successive overlapping five-year periods (i.e., 1926 to 1930, 1927 to 1931, etc.) for the same time period. We divided the annual returns into four categories:

1. Negative returns;

2. 0 to 10 percent returns;

3. 10 to 20 percent returns; and

4. Returns of more than 20 percent.

Figure 12.11.   Investment Returns for One- and Five-Year Time Horizons

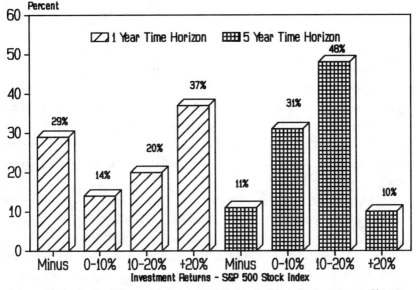

Source: *Stocks, Bonds, Bills, and Inflation 1991 Yearbook*, Ibbotson Associates, Chicago, IL, pp. 194–207. Computations by author.

For the entire period, the annual return on stocks averaged 10.1 percent. Focusing on a one-year time horizon (as shown by the four bars at the left side of the figure): approximately 29 percent of the time results would have been negative; about 33 percent between 0 and 20 percent; and about 37 percent of the time more than 20 percent. In short, about two-thirds of the time an investor would have been either very happy with the results, or very miserable and perhaps impelled to make some changes!

However, if a longer term perspective is taken, as shown by the bars on the right side of the figure, almost 80 percent of the time you would have received positive returns between 0 and 20 percent, and negative periods would have been reduced to about 11 percent of the total. A longer viewpoint is a lot easier for peace of mind.

RISK

Risk is an important concept in portfolio management, but it often is overlooked or only partly considered. For example, investors often say they don't want any "risky" investments. However, although "riskless" investments may avoid the loss of dollars, they also may not compensate for the loss of the purchasing power of those dollars because of the effects of inflation. Risk is often defined in terms of portfolio volatility, but in order to avoid volatility you may be assuming a bigger risk—the risk of not achieving the returns needed to reach your investment objectives.

One characteristic of risk, and one that often is the only kind of risk considered, is *volatility*. Volatility is defined as fluctuations in market price or in total investment return (income plus or minus market appreciation or depreciation of the investment). Volatility may be measured in absolute terms or relative to some market average. The investor should separate volatility into principal and income volatility and make a realistic appraisal of how much volatility can be tolerated in each. For example, if income is of primary importance, a fixed-income investment can be purchased and fluctuations in the value of the principal due to changes in the level of interest rates can be ignored. If volatility of principal cannot be tolerated, a short-term investment of the highest quality, such as a U.S. Treasury bill or a high-quality money-market fund is a preferable investment.

Volatility tolerance has two parts:

1. The practical effects that volatility will have on the ability to reach the investment objectives; and

2. The psychological effects of having a smaller investment fund than at sometime in the past.

The first part is significant because a financial cost is involved: the funds needed are not available. The second part may not be that critical. For example, if the primary need is income, some volatility in market principal may be tolerable so long as income is assured.

However, other kinds of risks should be considered:

Financial risk is the risk associated with a company itself, that is, a company cuts its dividend or files for bankruptcy, or a real estate venture goes sour.

Interest rate risk is associated with investments whose income is fixed by the terms of the security. When the coupon rate or the designated interest rate of an investment is fixed, changes in the general level of interest rates will cause the market value of the investment to rise or fall to adjust the actual yield on this investment to prevailing interest rates. Although the dollar income remains the same, the value of the principal of fixed-income investments will go up and down as interest rates rise and fall. An additional problem may occur when the security matures, because market yields at which reinvestment is made may be lower than they were when the investment was originally made. Many investors discovered this risk to their sorrow in the 1980s when high-yielding bank certificates of deposit had to be rolled over into lower yielding securities.

Purchasing power risk is the risk caused by the erosion in purchasing power due to the effects of inflation. Figure 3.4 shows the erosion in the purchasing power of $1 in 1950. By the end of 1990, it was worth only nineteen cents in 1950 purchasing power. This risk certainly is one that should be considered in establishing investment objectives.

Meeting Risk

In meeting risk, one fundamental factor should be kept in mind—the higher the expected return, the higher the risk. There is no free lunch. A high return is a good reflection of the risk assumed. A diversified portfolio reduces the risk of any one investment not living up to expectations.

Volatility risk is the most misunderstood, probably because investors get upset when the market value of their investments at some point in time is worth less than it was at an earlier date. In some portfolios, of course, volatility is undesirable. For example, a drop in the value of a participant's account in a profit-sharing plan a year or so before retirement can be a real problem. This risk could have been offset by gradually shifting more and more of the assets into cash equivalents as retirement approached.

Alternatively, consider a portion of a portfolio invested in diversified, well-selected common stocks with a history of and prospects for increasing earnings and dividends. This portfolio segment was designed to provide protection against inflation. Price volatility in the principal of this portfolio should cause little concern unless the principal will be needed to supplement income.

For *interest-rate risk,* the higher the quality of the security, the more likely it is to be affected by interest-rate risk rather than financial risk. Also the longer the maturity of the instrument, the greater the market volatility. An investor can seek protection against interest-rate risk by portfolio diversification and staggered fixed-income maturities.

Offsetting *purchasing power risk* depends on the type of inflation expected. A moderate inflation rate (say 5 percent or less a year) may be met with a diversified investment portfolio, including well-selected common stocks that have prospects for increasing earnings and dividends. In a higher and accelerating inflation, financial assets do poorly, as occurred during the 1970s. In that environment, the assets that did best were real estate and Treasury bills or other short-term money market instruments that adjust to inflation fairly quick.

THE ADVANTAGES OF PORTFOLIO DIVERSIFICATION

One of the important concepts of investment is the advantage of holding a portfolio of diversified securities. The concept of diversification is simple, summarized by the old adage, "Don't put all your eggs in one basket." Even safe investments such as Treasury bills provide a varying income stream over time as interest rates fluctuate, although the principal is always backed by the full taxing powers of the federal government. In addition, it is well-recognized that not all investments do equally well each year.

Table 12.3 illustrates the concept of diversification. The first column lists various types of fixed-income and equity investments. Treasury bills are used to represent conservative, short-term money-market investments such as certificates of deposit, savings accounts or money-market funds, which do not fluctuate in value and have a somewhat higher yield than Treasury bills. On a sum invested in guaranteed income contracts, insurance companies guarantee repayment of principal plus interest over a limited number of years, usually three or five.

The remainder of the table gives each type of investment a subjective grade, from A to D, based on how these investments have done in the past in terms of long-term investment returns, price volatility, inflation protection, and marketability. The grading is admittedly subjective and can be modified if wished. However, the main point derived from the table is that no investment receives a perfect score; one type of investment alone does not meet all investment requirements. Each type of investment has its advantages and disadvantages. Conse-

Table 12.3.
Types of Investments

Investment	Long-Term Total Investment Return	Price Volatility	Inflation Protection	Liquidity and Marketability
Fixed Income				
Treasury Bills	C	A	A	A
Intermediate Bonds	C	C	C	A
Long-Term Bonds	D	D	D	A
Mortgages	D	D	D	B
Guaranteed Income Contracts	C	A	D	D
Equity				
Stocks	B	C	C	A
Small Capitalization Stocks	A	D	B	B
Foreign Stocks	B	C	C	B
Real Estate	A	B	A	C
Oil and Gas	B	C	B	C

Grading Scale: A (most favorable) to D (least favorable).

quently, depending on the investor's objectives and circumstances, a blend of several investments is generally the best way to construct a portfolio.

Another way to look at diversification is illustrated in Table 12.4.

Some explanation of Table 12.4 is necessary. The returns are total returns (income plus appreciation), compounded for the 20-year period. The money-market fund was assumed to return about 0.5 percent per year above the Treasury bill rate. The high-grade bonds were represented by an index prepared by Salomon Brothers. Common stocks were represented by the Standard & Poor's 500 Stock Index.

For the diversified portfolio an initial diversification of 10 percent in a money-market fund is assumed—30 percent in high-grade bonds and 60 percent in stocks. Whatever the results in any year, the portfolio was rebalanced to the original diversification at the beginning of the next year. Essentially, this process reduced the more successful investments in any particular year and redistributed the proceeds among the less successful investments.

For each type of investment, the average yearly return is shown, as well as the fluctuations around that return (the standard deviation). The last column shows the standard devi-

Table 12.4.
Total Investment Return 1971–1990

Investment	Average Annual Return	Standard Deviation	Standard Deviation Divided by Average
Money-Market Fund	8.2%	2.6%	0.32
High-Grade Corporate Bonds	9.6	12.1	1.25
S&P 500 Stock Index	12.5	16.6	1.33
Diversified Portfolio	11.2	12.1	1.08

ation divided by the average, giving a measure of volatility risk per unit of return.

As one might expect, when moving from safe to riskier investments, the average return increases. However, so does the variations in the return around the average. What happens to a portfolio diversified among the three types of investments? Over time, the results of this portfolio fall between bonds and stocks, but the fluctuations per percentage point of return were reduced considerably and were less than for either stocks or bonds.

A balanced portfolio may not be for everyone. Some investors can't stand losses, even though they may be just on paper and not realized. These investors are willing to sacrifice the higher return from alternative investments for the assurance that the principal of their investments will always be safe. Other investors are risk-takers willing to assume the exposure to greater fluctuations in order to get the highest possible returns. Many others would prefer a higher return than that of money-market investment but also would like to control portfolio volatility. For that investor, a balanced portfolio, historically at least, has given a higher return than either Treasury bills or bonds and has had lower fluctuations than either an all-bond or an all-stock portfolio.

Types of Investments

Finally, in establishing investment objectives, consideration should be given to the types of investments preferred as well as to investments *not* liked and normally excluded from an investor's portfolio. Generally, an investor should understand and be comfortable with the investments chosen. At times, however, it may be worthwhile to be familiar with the characteristics of new investment vehicles that may enable the investor to reach the objectives more successfully. Referring again to

Table 12.3, the listed characteristics may be useful in considering the investments to include in a balanced portfolio.

FOLLOWING THE STOCK MARKET

Tracking interest rates is a relatively simple procedure, because both long and short rates are published daily in the financial press. Also, Chapter 11 referred to a St. Louis Federal Reserve Bank publication that provides such information on a weekly basis. Following stock prices, however, is a bit more difficult, because it involves selecting from among a number of indexes with varying characteristics. Which stock market average is best? A review of various stock price indexes and their construction may help answer these questions.

The Dow-Jones Average

Probably the best known average is the Dow-Jones Industrial Average. Although this average is probably the least useful, it is still the most popular because it goes back more than 100 years and is widely quoted in the financial press and the media.

The Dow-Jones Industrial Average represents only a small segment of the market. It is computed based on the daily prices of 30 stocks that account for about 20 percent of the market value of all of the stocks listed on the New York Stock Exchange. The index is biased toward heavy industry stocks; for example, two metal stocks (Bethlehem Steel and Alcoa), three international oil stocks (Exxon, Texaco, and Chevron), two chemical stocks (Du Pont and Union Carbide), two electrical equipment stocks (GE and Westinghouse), as well as giants such as General Motors, AT&T, IBM, MMM, Boeing, Sears, Kodak, and Proctor & Gamble. Consequently, movement of the prices of the Dow Industrials may often be different from the movement of the prices of a broad spectrum of NYSE stocks.

Another problem with the Dow arises from its method of construction. When the average first started, it was computed like any other average, that is, add up the prices of the 30 stocks and divide by 30. However, over time stocks were split, stock dividends were declared and some stocks were substituted for others. Each time that occurred, the *divisor*, which started out as 30, was changed so that, after adding up the prices of the 30 stocks and dividing by the divisor, the value of the average or index would be unchanged.

As a result of using this process over many years, the market value of the 30 stocks now is not divided by 30, but 0.505. Consequently, about a one-half point move in one of the 30 stocks can cause a one point move in the Dow! This computation method explains why the Dow index is so much larger than the price of any of the individual stocks in the average. It also explains the seemingly big daily movements of the average—far more than the changes in any component stock.

The Dow's method of computation gives heavier weight to stocks with larger dollar prices, and over the years the lowering of the divisor has distorted daily changes to make them almost meaningless. Moreover, if a stock were split, for example, 2 for 1, the stock suddenly has only half the importance it formerly had.

To get a better feel of the daily movements of individual stocks in the Dow, each day on the NYSE market price page, the *Wall Street Journal* prints a chart showing the daily high-low-close of the Dow averages for the past six months; on that same page yesterday's price change for each stock in the average is also reported.

Dow Jones averages are also computed in the same manner for 20 transportation stocks, 25 utility stocks and than a composite for all 65 stocks. The divisors for all indexes are printed daily in the *Wall Street Journal.*

Standard & Poor's Indexes

Among the more widely used price indexes are those prepared by Standard & Poor's Corporation. These indexes are probably the ones most widely used by professional investors because of their long history and also the breadth and depth of their coverage.

Standard & Poor's prepares a composite of the prices of 500 stocks, including 400 industrial, 20 transport, 40 utility, and 40 financial stocks, which is reported daily in the financial section of most newspapers. Most of the stocks in the indexes are listed on the various stock exchanges, although some stocks traded over-the-counter are included.

The composite price index goes back to 1918, although it included only 90 stocks until 1957. It has also been linked to an older index prepared by the Cowles Commission, so that a continuous record of stock prices is available going back to 1871. Information on the industry indexes are reported from 1918.

The Standard & Poor's weekly publication, *The Outlook,* (available in many public libraries), reports the values of more than 100 industry components in addition to the weekly values of the broad indexes. Consequently, these indexes are used more than any others to follow the movement of industry groups. However, Dow-Jones has recently introduced industry indexes of its own, which are published daily in the *Wall Street Journal.*

The computation of the Standard & Poor's data is by market weight, that is, the market price of each stock is multiplied by the number of shares outstanding. The totals for all stocks are then added and reported relative to the value in a

base period (1941 to 1943), with the base period set equal to 10.
The recent value of the composite index of about 350 means
that the value of the stocks in the index is about 35 times the
average value in 1941 to 1943. No adjustment is needed for
stock splits, because a split does not affect the market value of
all of the shares of the company. Changes resulting from
mergers, delistings, substitutions, or rights offerings are adjusted for by a proportionate change in the base value.

The average now accounts for about 80 percent of the
value of the stocks listed on the NYSE, including all of the
stocks in the Dow. Companies that have a large number of
shares, that is, large capitalization stocks, or industries with
large capitalization stocks (e.g., office equipment, oils, drugs,
and telecommunications), dominate the movements of the index. A comparison of the Dow and the Standard & Poor's
indexes for the past 15 years is shown on Figure 12.12. Both

Figure 12.12.   Dow-Jones Industrials vs. S&P 500 Stock Index

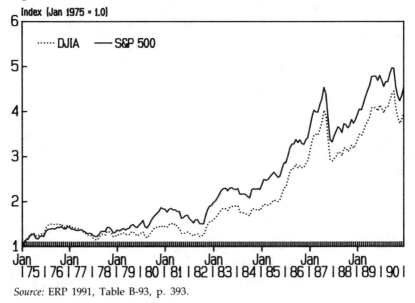

Source: ERP 1991, Table B-93, p. 393.

indexes were made equal to 1 for January 1975, so that their subsequent changes can be compared easily. Growth of the Standard & Poor's clearly has been greater than that of the Dow since 1977, and the Standard & Poor's has been somewhat more volatile.

The New York Stock Exchange Index

The New York Stock Exchange publishes a daily index that reflects the prices of all of the roughly 1,500 stocks listed on the Exchange, as well as indexes of divisions of these stocks into industrial, transportation, utility, and financial stocks. The index goes back to 1964, and it can be extended back further to 1939 by linking it to a now-discontinued index once prepared by the Securities and Exchange Commission (SEC).

The NYSE indexes are constructed in the same manner as the Standard & Poor's indexes. However, the base period is market value on December 31, 1965, and the base is set at 50, which was reasonably close to the average value of all NYSE stocks on the base date. Because all NYSE-listed stocks are included, changes occur more frequently than for the Standard & Poor's composite index.

The NYSE index is more comprehensive than the Standard & Poor's index in one way because it covers all of the stocks listed on the NYSE. However, it does not cover stocks listed on other exchanges or stocks that are not listed. Because it is constructed in the same way as the Standard & Poor's, it is also dominated by the movement of large capitalization stocks.

Other Indexes

The *American Stock Exchange (AMEX) index* reflects the price movements of all stocks traded on the AMEX as well as American depository receipts of foreign companies traded on the AMEX. These companies are smaller than the companies listed on the NYSE. The index is constructed in the same way as the Standard & Poor's indexes. The index goes back to the beginning of 1969 but has a base level set at 100 on August 31, 1973.

The price movements of *over-the-counter stocks* traded through the *National Association of Securities Dealers Automated Quotation System* (NASDAQ) are reflected in an index that covers about 4,700 stocks. The index and seven subindexes are computed like the Standard & Poor's indexes, that is, total market-value weighted, with the base period of February 5, 1971, set at 100. The principal difference between this index and those mentioned earlier is that prices used are not transaction prices but median bid prices of the market vendors during the day at the time the index is computed. A small number of large capitalization stocks have a significant influence on movements of this index.

The *Value Line Composite Index* is comprised of prices of about 1,700 NYSE and non-NYSE stocks covered in the Value Line Investment Service. The calculations are based on daily percentage changes, so that each stock receives the same weight in the calculation of the index, regardless of the company size or market capitalization. Consequently, its movements can be compared with the market-value weighted indexes to compare the movements of large versus smaller capitalization stocks. The base period and starting point for the index is June 1961. Daily price changes are reported in the *Wall Street Journal* and other financial papers, but historical data must be obtained from Value Line.

The *Wilshire 5,000 Equity Index* is the most comprehensive index available. It now covers about 5,700 common stocks and includes all stocks traded on the NYSE, AMEX and those included in the NASDAQ index. The construction is the same as the construction of the S&P indexes. Month-end prices are available for this index since 1971, and the index is based on the December 31, 1980 capitalization of the market, which was $1,404 billion.

Which Index to Use?

With so many indexes to choose from, which one should be used? Some guidelines to follow:

Although the Dow often is used to reflect day-to-day stock price changes, it is not representative of the broad market. Its method of construction is unusual, so that changes in the Dow's raw numbers give an exaggerated and at times an inaccurate idea of the general movement of stock prices;

The Standard & Poor's indexes are widely used because of their broader coverage, long history, and many subindexes. The NYSE index is an even broader measure of NYSE-listed stocks than is the Standard & Poor's. The AMEX and the NASDAQ reflect movements of their respective markets and the different types of stocks traded on them. The Wilshire 5,000 is the most comprehensive index available but does not yet have industry components, nor is it as well-known as the others.

The Standard & Poor's, NYSE, AMEX, NASDAQ, and Wilshire indexes are all weighted by the price of individual stocks times the number of shares, and therefore larger capitalization stocks have a greater impact on price changes. An unweighed index, such as the Value Line Index, can provide another view and permit comparison of movements of smaller versus larger capitalized stocks.

Daily percentage changes in the various indexes provide a better way to compare the movements of the indexes and the different views they present of the market. Such percentage changes can be found every day on the market price page of the *Wall Street Journal*.

No one average is good for all purposes. Select an average that will answer particular questions about the movement of broad stock aggregates. It is strongly recommended that price movements be viewed over periods of months and years, rather than too intense a focus on day-to-day price fluctuations.

SUMMARY

The most important step in managing an investment portfolio is to establish a clearly defined set of investment objectives. These objectives include describing the purpose for which the portfolio was established, determining an absolute rate of return needed to meet these objectives, deciding whether this return is realistic by comparing it with historical rates of return for similar investments, and establishing the risk tolerance for the portfolio. Portfolio risk includes more than just price volatility of the portfolio; financial risk, interest rate risk, and purchasing power risk should also be considered. One way of partially offsetting these various types of risk is through a diversified portfolio of securities. Various price indexes are used to follow security price movements. The appropriate index depends on the purpose for which measurement is made.

References

This section provides the sources for each of the charts and tables in the various chapters. Certain references are used repeatedly so they are described at the beginning of the reference list together with an abbreviation that will subsequently be used to identify them. These reports are all discussed in Chapter 11, including where they may be obtained.

SCB—*Survey of Current Business*, Bureau of Economic Analysis, U.S. Department of Commerce

ERP—*Economic Report of the President*

NIPA—*The National Income and Product Accounts of the United States, 1929–82*

BS—*Business Statistics, 1961–88*

Chapter 1

Figure 1.1. *GNP and Profits.*
Source: Current data for GNP: SCB, February 1991, Table 1.1, p. 7. Profits: SCB, February 1991, Table 1.14, p. 9. Earlier data ERP 1991, Table B-1, p. 286 and Table B-24, p. 313.

Figure 1.2. *S&P Earnings and Prices.*
Source: Standard & Poor's Trade and Statistics Manual, Standard & Poor's Corporation, New York, NY, ps. 1, 115–118.

Figure 1.3. *Stock P/E Ratios and Inflation.*
Source: P/E ratios: Same as Figure 1.2. CPI: ERP 1991, Table B-62, p. 356.

Figure 1.4. *Short- and Long-Term Interest Rates.*
Source: ERP 1991, Table B-71, p. 368.

Figure 1.5. *Interest Rates and Inflation.*
Source: ERP 1991, Table B-71, p. 368; Table B-62, p. 356.

Chapter 2

Figure 2.1. *Real Gross National Product Percent Change.*
Source: SCB, February 1991, Table 1.2, p. 7; earlier data ERP 1991, Table B-5, p. 293.

Table 2.1. *How GNP Was Taken Off the Market—1990.*
Source: SCB, February 1991, Table 1.1, p. 7.

Table 2.2. *GNP for 1990 in Current and Constant 1982 Dollars.*
Source: SCB, February 1991, Table 1.1, Table 1.2, p. 7.

Table 2.3. *Income Distribution of GNP—1990.*
Source: SCB, February 1991, Table 1.9, Table 1.14, p. 9.

Chapter 3

Figure 3.1. *Prices and Wages.*
Source: Hourly compensation: U.S. Department of Labor, Bureau of Labor Statistics release *Productivity and Costs,* various dates. CPI: ERP 1991, Table B-61, p. 355.

Figure 3.2. *Components of Consumer Price Index.*
Source: CPI Detailed Report, U.S. Department of Labor, Bureau of Labor Statistics, December 1990, p. 62.

Figure 3.3. *Consumer Price Index 1950–90.*
Source: ERP 1991, Table B-60, p. 354. Computations author.

Figure 3.4. *Purchasing Power of a 1950 Dollar.*
Source: ERP 1991, Table B-60, p. 354. Computations by author.

Figure 3.5. *CPI versus PPI versus GNP Deflator.*
Source: ERP 1991, Table B-62, p. 356; Table B-66, page 3; Table B-5, p. 293.

Chapter 4

Figure 4.1. *Personal Income—1990.*
Source: SCB, February 1991, Table 2.1, p. 11.

Figure 4.2. *Change in Employees on Nonaq Payrolls.*
Source: SCB, February 1991, p. S-10; data prior to December 1989 obtained directly from BLS.

Figure 4.3. *Percent Change in Personal Income and Expenditures.*
Source: SCB, February 1991, p. S-1; earlier data from SCB February 1990, p. S-1; BS, p. 1–2.

Figure 4.4. *Personal Consumption Expenditures.*
Source: 1990 data from SCB, February 1991, Table 1.1, p. 7; 1950 data from NIPA, Table 1.1, p. 7.

Figure 4.5. *PCE—Durables.*
Source: 1990 data from SCB, Table 2.2, p. 11; 1950 data from NIPA, Table 2.2, p. 99.

Figure 4.6. *PCE—Nondurables.*
Source: Same as Figure 4.5.

Figure 4.7. *PCE—Services.*
Source: Same as Figure 4.5.

Figure 4.8. *Automobile Sales—Domestic and Imports.*
Source: SCB, February 1991, p. S-32; earlier issues of SCB for data prior to December 1989.

Figure 4.9. *Retail Sales—1989.*
Source: SCB, February 1991, ps. 8–9.

Figure 4.10. *Retail Sales—Monthly Percent Change.*
Source; SCB, February 1991, p. S-8; earlier data direct from Bureau of Census.

Figure 4.11. *Retail Sales—Monthly Percent Change Durables and Nondurables*
Source: Same as for Figure 4.10.

Figure 4.12. *Housing Starts and Building Permits.*
Source: ERP 1991, Table B-53, p. 346; data for 1987–88 from earlier ERP.

Figure 4.13. *Personal Savings Rate.*
Source: ERP 1991, Table B-26, p. 316.

Figure 4.14. *Consumer Installment Credit as a Percent of Personal Income.*
Source: SCB, February 1991, p. C-4; SCB October 1990, p. C-40.

Figure 4.15. *Consumer Confidence and Expectations.*
Source: SCB, February 1991, p. C-2; earlier data direct from Bureau of Economic Analysis, Department of Commerce.

Table 4.1. *Relationship of National Income and Personal Income—1990.*
Source: SCB, February 1991, Table 1.9, p. 9.

Table 4.2. *Personal Income and Personal Savings—1990.*
Source: SCB, February 1991, Table 2.1, p. 11.

Table 4.3. *Sources and Uses of Savings—1990.*
Source: SCB, February 1991, Table 1.1, p. 7, and Table 5.1, p. 14.

Chapter 5

Figure 5.1. *Nonresidential Fixed Investment as a Percent GNP.*
Source: SCB, February 1991, Table 1.1, p. 7; ERP 1991, Table B-1, p. 286.

Figure 5.2. *Nonresidential Fixed Investment Distribution.*
Source: SCB, February 1991, Table 5.12, p. 16; 1950 data NIPA, Table 5.5, 5.6, p. 231, 233.

Figure 5.3. *Nondefense Capital Goods—New Orders and Shipments.*
Source: SCB, February 1991, p. S-4. SCB earlier issues for earlier data.

Figure 5.4. *Nondefense Capital Goods—Inventory and Backlog Ratios.*
Source: Same as Table 5.3. Computations by author.

Figure 5.5. *Total Industry Capacity Utilization.*
Source: SCB, February 1991, p. C-2; earlier data *Federal Reserve Bulletin,* June 1990, p. 433.

Figure 5.6. *Nonresidential Fixed Investment versus Corporate Cash Flow.*
Source: Nonresidential Fixed Investment: ERP 1991, Table B-1, p. 286. Corporate Cash Flow: SCB February 1991, Table 1.14, p. 9; earlier data in earlier issues of SCB and NIPA, Table 1.14 ps. 47–48.

Figure 5.7. *Changes in Business Inventories—1982 dollars.*
Source: SCB, February 1991, Tables 1, 2, p. 7; earlier data in earlier issues of SCB, and NIPA, p. 283.

Figure 5.8. *Real GNP and Final Sales Percent Change.*
Source: SCB, February 1991, Table 8.1, p. 20; earlier data in earlier issues of SCB.

Figure 5.9. *Change in Business Sales and Inventories.*
Source: SCB, February 1991, ps. S-2, S-3; earlier data direct from Bureau of Economic Analysis, U.S. Department of Commerce. Computations by author.

Figure 5.10. *Ratios of Inventories to Sales.*
Source: Same as Figure 5.9.

Figure 5.11. *Percent Change in Industrial Production Index.*
Source: SCB, February 1991, p. S-1; earlier data in earlier issues of SCB and BS, p. 3.

Figure 5.12. *Purchasing Managers' Index.*
Source: Direct from National Association of Purchasing Management, Tempe, AZ; latest data as reported in *Wall Street Journal.*

Figure 5.13. *Durable Goods New Orders.*
Source: SCB, February 1991, p. S-4; earlier data from earlier issues of SCB and BS, p. 229.

Chapter 6

Figure 6.1. *U.S. Balance on Current Account.*
Source: ERB 1991, Table B-102, p. 402.

Figure 6.2. *Exports and Imports as a Percent GNP.*
Source: SCB, February 1991, Table 1.1, p. 7; earlier data ERP 1991, Table B-1, ps. 286–287.

Figure 6.3. *Net Exports of Goods and Services.*
Source: SCB, February 1991, Table 1.1, p. 7; earlier data ERP 1991, Table B-1, p. 287, BS, ps. 276–277.

Figure 6.4. *Monthly Merchandise Trade Deficit.*
Source: SCB, February 1991, ps. S-16, S-17; earlier data direct from the Bureau of the Census, U.S. Department of Commerce.

Figure 6.5. *U.S. Merchandise Exports 1970 versus 1989.*
Source: ERP, 1991, Table B-103, p. 404.

Figure 6.6. *U.S. Merchandise Imports 1970 versus 1989.*
Source: Same as Figure 6.5.

Figure 6.7. *Asset Flows from and to the United States.*
Source: ERP 1991, Table B-102, p. 403.

Figure 6.8. *U.S. International Investment Position.*
Source: SCB, June 1990, Table 1, p. 55.

Figure 6.9. *Foreign versus U.S. Direct Investments.*
Source: Same as Figure 6.8.

Figure 6.10. *Exchange Value of the U.S. Dollar.*
Source: SCB, February 1991, p. C-5; earlier data from Federal Reserve Board Division of Research and Statistics.

Chapter 7

Figure 7.1. *Government Purchases of Goods and Services as a Percent of GNP.*
Source: SCB, February 1991, Table 1.1, p. 7; earlier data, ERP 1991, Table B-1, p. 287. Computations by author.

Figure 7.2. *Government Expenditures as a Percent of GNP.*
Source: SCB, February 1991, Table 1.1, p. 7; Tables 3.2, 3.3, p. 12; earlier data, ERP 1991, Table B-79, p. 379.

Figure 7.3. *Federal Receipts and Expenditures.*
Source: Same as Figure 7.2.

Figure 7.4. *State and Local Receipts and Expenditures.*
Source: Same as Figure 7.2.

Figure 7.5. *Federal Debt—Total and as a Percent of GNP.*
Source: ERP 1991, Table B-76, p. 375.

Figure 7.6. *OASI and DI Income and Outgo.*
Source: Budget of the U.S. Government, Fiscal Year 1992, Part Seven, Table 13.1, ps. 165–171.

Figure 7.7. *Social Security Trust Fund Balance.*
Source: 1990 Annual Report of the Federal Old-Age and Survivors Insurance and Disability Insurance Trust Funds, Table F3, Alternative II-B, p. 135.

Figure 7.8. *Hospital Insurance Income and Outgo.*
Source: Same as Figure 7.6.

Figure 7.9. *Medical Insurance Income and Outgo.*
Source: Same as Figure 7.6.

Table 7.1. *Federal Government Receipts and Expenditures.*
Source: Same as Figure 7.2.

Table 7.2. *State and Local Receipts and Expenditures.*
Source: Same as Figure 7.2.

Chapter 8

Figure 8.1. *Federal Funds and the Discount Rate.*
Source: ERP 1991, Table B-71, ps. 368–369.

Figure 8.2. *M2 Money Supply, 1989–91.*
Source: Current data: Federal Reserve Data, *Wall Street Journal*, every Friday; earlier data, SCB, February 1991, pg. S-15; ERP 1991, Table B-67, p. 363; target ranges from *Federal Reserve Bulletin*, March 1991, Table 1, p. 148.

Figure 8.3. *Yield Curve, February 13, 1991*
Source: Prices from *Wall Street Journal*, "Treasury Bonds, Notes and Bills," February 13, 1991.

Figure 8.6. *Bond Maturity Yield Spreads, 1987–91*
Source: Current data: *Economic Indicators*, February 1991, p. 30; earlier data, ERP 1991, Table B-71, p. 368.

Figure 8.7. *Bond Quality Yield Spreads, 1987–91*
Source: Same as Figure 8.6.

Chapter 9

Figure 9.1. *Actual and Potential Real Output 1954–90.*
Source: Actual Output: SCB, February 1991, Table 1.1, p. 7; earlier data, ERP 1991, Table B-1, p. 286; potential output direct from Congressional Budget Office.

Figure 9.2. *Consumer Price Index 1860–1990.*
Source: Data for 1946–90: ERP 1991, Table B-58, p. 351; earlier data from *Long Term Economic Growth 1860–1970*, ps. 222–223, Bureau of Economic Analysis, U.S. Department of Commerce, Washington, D.C., June 1973. Computations by author.

Figure 9.3. *CPI With and Without Food and Energy.*
Source: ERP 1991, Table B-61, p. 355.

Figure 9.4. *Annual Change in Real Compensation per hour.*
Source: ERP 1991, Table B-47, p. 399.

Figure 9.5. Cyclical Indicators.
Source: SCB, March 1991, p. C-7.

Chapter 10

Figure 10.1. *NIPA Corporate Profits.*
Source: ERP 1991, Table B-24, p. 313.

Figure 10.2. *Capital Consumption Adjustment and Inventory Valuation Adjustment.*
Source: Same as Figure 10.1.

Figure 10.3. *Rest of World Corporate Profits.*
Source: ERP 1991, Table B-89, p. 389.

Figure 10.4. *Output, Hours, and Productivity.*
Source: Productivity and Costs, Bureau of Labor Statistics releases, quarterly.

Figure 10.5. *Factors Affecting Labor Costs.*
Source: Same as Figure 10.4

Figure 10.6. *Unit Labor and Nonlabor Costs.*
Source: Same as Figure 10.4.

Figure 10.7. *Total Unit Costs and Prices.*
Source: Same as Figure 10.4.

Figure 10.8. *Percent Distribution Nonfinancial Corp Costs and Profits.*
Source: SCB, February 1991, Table 7.18, p. 19; earlier data from SCB, July 1982 through July 1990; and BS, Table 7.18.

Figure 10.9. *Nonfinancial Profits as a Percent of GNP.*
Source: SCB, February 1991, Table 1.1, Table 1.16, ps. 7, 10; earlier data from SCB, July 1982 through July 1990 and BS, Tables 1.1, 1.16. Computations by author.

Table 10.1. *Corporate Profit Components—1990.*
Source: SCB, February 1991, Tables 1.16, 6.18 B, ps. 10, 16. Computations by author.

Table 10.2. *Nonfinancial Corporate Unit Costs and Profits—1990.*
Source: SCB, February 1991, Table 1.16, p. 10.

Chapter 12

The data from all but one figure and all tables were taken from *Stocks, Bonds, Bills, and Inflation 1991 Yearbook,* Exhibits C-2–C-8, ps. 194–207. This book is published by Ibbotson Associates, 8 South Michigan Avenue, Suite 700, Chicago, IL. Computations by author.

Chart 12.12. *Dow-Jones Industrials versus S&P 500 Index.*
Source: ERP 1991, Table B-93, p. 393.

Index